PROCUREMENT OF SERVICES IN THE PUBLIC SECTOR

THE BIDDER'S PERSPECTIVE

David Marcer

First edition published by Cambridge Academic, The Studio, High Green, Gt. Shelford, Cambridge CB22 5EG.

ISBN 1-903-499-74-7
978-1-903499-74-0

Printed and bound in the United Kingdom by
4edge Ltd, 7a Eldon Way Industrial Estate, Hockley, Essex, SS5 4AD.

Contents

Preface	i
Introduction	1
Some definitions	1
What are the Regulations about?	3
What are the qualifying thresholds?	4
What procedure will be followed?	5
What is most economically advantageous tender?	6
What are Part B services?	7
Where can I find out about upcoming procurements of public sector services?	8
How do I apply to become a bidder?	9
What is a procurement hub?	10
The context of procurement	11
What are PQQs and ITTs?	16
What is an electronic procurement system?	17
How can I get more information?	19
What is a clarification process?	21
What are Selection and Award?	23
Is there a continuum from PQQ to ITT?	24
Are purchasers obliged to tell you their budgetary limit or price ceiling?	24
Who can see my bid?	25
What if I miss something from a response?	27
Can I negotiate in a procurement process?	28
Elephant traps	30
Past performance	31
How does evaluation work?	33
How do evaluators work?	34
Will something said in one answer be taken into account in another?	35
What are evaluation criteria? Can I see them?	35
How does short-listing work?	38
How is the winning tender chosen?	41
Evaluating more complex bid prices	43
How do I price my bid?	45
Risk sharing – what is that about?	47
Performance indicators	48
The problem with questions	52
Bidder presentations – what are they for?	53
What really counts?	55
New entrants	57
Who is the bidder?	59
TUPE	61
Bidding against an incumbent supplier	62
Bidding as an incumbent provider	63
If I lose a procurement can I charge for my wasted time?	66

What can I do if a procurement is abandoned? 66
What is a framework agreement? 67
The shift in the balance of power 69
Challenging procurements 70
Some technicalities concerning contracts 81
Responding to PQQS and ITTs 86
Can I leave my response to the last minute? 89
In conclusion 90

Bibliography 91
Index 97

Dedicated to the memory of my late father Ted Marcer who missed the opportunity to proof-read and edit my writing.

Thanks to my wife Lynne for her help and forbearance.

Preface

Much has been written about the public procurement process. For the most part these words have been aimed at the purchaser and set out how things must be done according to the law. As in most walks of life however what must be done is not necessarily what is done.

In this book the author outlines those aspects of the public procurement regulations that are directly relevant to a bidder taking part in a procurement for the supply of public services and draws on his experience of advising on procurement in central government, local government and the NHS to reveal what actually happens in practice.

Although aimed primarily at small to medium enterprises in the health sector, most of what is said in this book is of interest to bidders for service contracts in any part of the public sector.

Introduction

The regulations governing public sector procurement (hereinafter called the *Regulations*) bear mainly on the purchaser. In theory the purchaser consults the Regulations and designs a procurement process that complies with them, then bidders follow the process and that is compliance taken care of, but:

- the complexity of the Regulations (and more particularly the case law that has developed around them) means that it cannot be taken for granted that a purchaser has a good grasp of the law;
- despite being highly prescriptive in some areas, the Regulations allow considerable latitude in others; and
- observing the Regulations alone is insufficient to guarantee either a good procurement process or a good bid.

If you are to maximise your chances of success you need a basic grasp of the Regulations, but more importantly you need to understand how purchasers think and operate, especially in those parts of the process of which the Regulations say little. There can be no guarantee that by following the advice in this book you will win more bids, but it should certainly reduce your odds in the procurement sweepstake.

Somewhere in what follows you will find the following caveat: *the above advice is (more or less) appropriate for a rational purchaser, but not all purchasers act rationally*. This might be the theme of this book. The author has attempted to distinguish between what ought to happen and what might or does happen. Even so the golden rule for bidders in public procurements is, and always will be, *caveat vendor*.

It is difficult to be prescriptive about procurement law and in the nature of things practice differs from purchaser to purchaser, so the words 'generally', 'usually' and other such usages occur more than the author would wish. Even when they aren't used don't assume a statement is universally true; nevertheless it is to be hoped that this book generates more light than heat.

Some definitions

In so far as is possible jargon has been kept to a minimum, but a few definitions are required:

- ***Contract notice*** is the notice (often called advertisement) appearing in the OJEU (see below) in which the procurement is announced and which invites expressions of interest from prospective bidders.
- ***Contract award notice*** is the notice appearing in the OJEU in which the purchaser announces the result of the procurement process.
- ***ITT*** is an Invitation to Tender.
- ***OJEU*** is the Official Journal of the European Union. Strictly speaking notices are published in the *Supplement to the Official Journal of the European Union* (*S series*, *Official Journal S* or *OJ S*), but it is always referred to as the OJEU.
- ***PQQ*** is a Pre-qualification Questionnaire.
- ***Purchaser*** means the public sector organisation procuring the services.

In the Regulations various words are used for supplier-side participants according to their status and the stage of the process. Such precise distinctions aren't really necessary here, so we use the following:

- ***Prospective bidder*** is a person or organisation who is considering taking part in, has expressed an interest in or is participating in the PQQ process.
- ***Bidder*** strictly means a person or organisation who has been shortlisted following the PQQ stage, but when the context allows bidder is used to mean a participant at any stage in the process.
- ***Supplier*** is also used to describe a participant or prospective participant where it best suits the context.
- ***Contractor*** is the person or organisation who has been awarded the contract.

The words ***bid*** and ***tender*** are interchangeable and mean a bidder's response[1] to an ITT, i.e. a document that includes a price.

- ***Response*** is used as a general term for a bidder's reply to either a PQQ or an ITT.

1. It is often erroneously said that prospective bidders 'submit a PQQ' and then 'submit an ITT'. No, the bidder submits a response to a PQQ and (unsurprisingly) submits a tender in response to an Invitation to Tender.

- ***Regulations*** are the European Public Procurement Regulations. For convenience, unless the context implies otherwise, we include in this definition the developing body of case law on public procurement. European regulations are incorporated into English law in the form of Statutory Instruments, the principal one concerning public procurement being the Public Contracts Regulations 2006[2]. Apart from strings of initials in this book only this term – *Regulations* – is blessed with a capital letter when it doesn't start a sentence.
- ***Supply/ies*** is Eurospeak for goods.
- ***Works*** is Eurospeak for building work, civil engineering, etc.

What are the Regulations about?

This book is not a tutorial on the Regulations – there are already plenty of those in circulation, but in brief[3]:

- all procurements of goods and services by public sector and utility[4] organisations in the European Union are subject to the Regulations;
- the Regulations describe procedures to be followed by purchasers according to the value and nature of what is being procured;
- the overarching principles of public procurement are derived from the Treaty of Rome. They are set out in Regulation 4(3) of the Public Contracts Regulations 2006 and are: *equitable treatment, non-discrimination and transparency*.

  Equity and non-discrimination are a little difficult to distinguish one from another, which perhaps explains why they are bundled together in the Regulations. Taken together they mean, for example, that all bidders and prospective bidders must be supplied with the same information about the requirement and that the purchaser cannot arbitrarily exclude a supplier or class of suppliers.

---

2. http://www.legislation.gov.uk/uksi/2006/5/contents/made – is the statutory instrument that covers most of the Regulations, but there are others that we refer to later.
3. For those who wish to know more about procurement law and policy the EU Simap website is a useful source: http://simap.europa.eu/. This website has the advantage of being a constant presence whereas UK government websites tend to change as governments reorganise departmental structures. Currently the Cabinet Office deals with EU procurement: http://procurement.cabinetoffice.gov.uk/policy-capability/latest-policy-and-regulations/public-procurement-policy.
4. i.e. water, electricity, gas, railways, etc for which the rules differ in some areas and which are not further discussed in this book.

Transparency means what it says – all dealings and decisions must be open and above board, and open to public scrutiny[5];

- in addition to the Regulations there is a growing body of case law, most of it referring to the overarching principles; and
- all public procurements must begin with a widely publicised advertisement (which generally means a notice in the OJEU) and follow one of the procedures defined in the Regulations.

What are the qualifying thresholds?

The Regulations govern all public procurement, but only those contracts with a value above certain thresholds need to follow the formal procedures[6] (i.e. beginning with a notice in the OJEU). The values differ according to the nature of what is being purchased, and there are other complicating factors, but in essence the thresholds are as follows.

Contracts awarded by central government departments and agencies:

Supplies	£113,057 (€ 130,000)
Services	£113,057 (€130,000)
Works	£4,348,350 (€5,000,000)

Contracts awarded by other public bodies:

Supplies	£173,934 (€200,000)
Services	£173,934 (€200,000)
Works	£4,348,350 (€5,000,000)

These values are net of VAT.

In most circumstances it will be obvious whether the likely value of a contract will exceed the threshold, but in marginal cases purchasers are obliged to make fair estimates rather than ducking under the threshold by estimating what a 'competitive' bid would cost.

In the same spirit 'disaggregation' or splitting up a contract into several parts so that each comes under the threshold is not allowed.

The value of a contract for services is the total cost over the life of the

5. But, as we shall see later, not completely.

6. But even where the formal procedures are not followed the three principles of equitable treatment, non-discrimination and transparency still apply (although how they can be enforced is another matter).

contract or, if shorter than four years, 48 times the monthly cost. The thresholds are widely publicised on the web sites of the many organisations that offer advice on procurement and are hidden away on the Cabinet Office website[7].

What procedure will be followed?

The Regulations define four procedures:

- **Open procedure** – effectively tenders are submitted by all-comers without any short-listing. This procedure is probably best fitted to the procurement of supplies that can be unambiguously defined and which have few differentiating features (e.g. large quantities of grey paint);
- **Restricted procedure** – restricted because the submission of tenders is limited to those bidders who have qualified for an initial shortlist. By limiting numbers purchasers can demand and process more information in the tenders;
- **Competitive dialogue** – where a solution is developed through a series of discussions between purchaser and short-listed bidders. The use of this procedure is restricted to *particularly complex projects*[8] where there is some uncertainty about the nature of the solution prior to the procurement; and
- **Negotiated procedure** – where negotiation does actually take place. This procedure, however, may only be used in very particular circumstances and is unusual.

The Restricted procedure is the most commonly used procedure for the procurement of services in the public sector, so from now on we are talking almost exclusively about procurement under this procedure (and furthermore where the contract is awarded on the basis of *most economically advantageous tender* – an explanation of which appears below). The main stages of the Restricted procedure are as follows:

- the purchaser publishes a notice in the OJEU asking for expressions of interest from prospective bidders;

7. http://procurement.cabinetoffice.gov.uk/policy-capability/latest-policy-and-regulations/public-procurement-policy
8. Regulation 18 of the Public Contracts Regulations 2006

- a PQQ is issued to suppliers who have expressed an interest;
- responses to the PQQ are evaluated, a short-list is drawn up and those who have submitted a PQQ are informed of the outcome;
- an ITT is issued to short-listed bidders;
- bidders submit tenders in response to the ITT;
- tenders are evaluated and a successful bidder is selected;
- unsuccessful bidders are informed and told why they were not chosen;
- the contract is signed; and
- services commence.

The Regulations impose no overall time limit on a procurement, but there are intermediate time limits, the significant ones being the time allowed for expressions of interest following publication of the notice (37 calendar days, but fewer in certain circumstances) and the time to submit a tender following receipt of the ITT (40 calendar days, but fewer in certain circumstances).

As a general rule a procurement under the Restricted procedure will take around six months from publication of the notice to award of contract, but shortage of resources or indecision on the part of the purchaser can extend the process.

- ***It is only rarely that procurements for the supply of services follow any procedure other than Restricted. Any prospective bidder faced with an alternative procedure should proceed carefully and if necessary take legal advice.***
- ***Be particularly careful where competitive dialogue is proposed. Is the project really 'particularly complex' and the solution uncertain or is this just a purchaser who can't be bothered to put the work into defining the requirement? Think carefully before you get involved in what might turn out to be a fishing expedition.***

What is most economically advantageous tender?

The Regulations define two bases for awarding the contract: *most economically advantageous tender*[9] and *lowest price*. Most economically

9. Often the acronym MEAT is used, but out of respect for vegetarians it will not be used here.

advantageous tender is what most people mean when they say best value for money, i.e. a combination of price and other factors.

These other factors are set out in the Regulations[10] as follows: *A contracting authority shall use criteria linked to the subject matter of the contract to determine that an offer is the most economically advantageous including quality, price, technical merit, aesthetic and functional characteristics, environmental characteristics, running costs, cost effectiveness, after sales service, technical assistance, delivery date and delivery period and period of completion.*

It is not compulsory for purchasers to examine every one of these factors, and because this is a general purpose clause covering both supplies and services not all the factors listed are necessarily characteristics of a service.

In general purchasers tend to lump these other factors together and refer to them all as *quality*, so a bidder's *quality score* is the score awarded to the bid for answers to questions other than that/those about price.

The basis for award is stated in the Contract Notice and for service procurements it will almost always be most economically advantageous tender. Ways of combining quality and price to arrive at this result are discussed later in this book.

What are Part A and Part B services?

The Regulations specify two classes of services which are set out in the Regulations in lists known as Part A and Part B[11]. The procedural rules set out in the Regulations apply in full to the procurement of services in Part A, but only two relatively minor rules apply to the services in Part B, which is where health services lie.

Why then do procurements of health services usually follow the whole of the Regulations? The answer is that until relatively recently no one was

10. Regulation 30(2) of the Public Contracts Regulations 2006

11. Part A contains the majority of services and includes things such as computer services, accounting services, advertising, telecommunications and air transport. Part B includes health, education, legal services, rail transport and (the author's favourite) investigation and security services, except armoured car services. It is said that there is a major and minor aspect to the split and that Part B services, as well as being minor, are only of interest to bidders within the country where they are to be delivered. But 'minor' is a strange classification when the NHS is second only in number of employees to Indian Railways (or the Army of the People's Republic of China, or whatever is the latest comparator) and that health contracts can be worth many millions of pounds.

too bothered because piecemeal commissioning of consequently low value contracts wasn't really seen as public procurement. Now that the outsourcing of health services has become more common, however, lawyers are looking further than the letter of the Regulations to the overarching principles of equitable treatment, non-discrimination and transparency.

Put simply, current legal opinion is that, regardless of the Part B exception, the principles demand that a procurement of health services must be openly advertised. It follows that the safest way to satisfy this requirement is to advertise in the OJEU; furthermore, the safest (and easiest) way to ensure compliance with the principles as the procurement proceeds is to follow the Regulations.

So although health services fall in Part B, purchasers increasingly act as if they fall in Part A, and (this is an important point for bidders) if the purchaser adopts procedures appropriate to Part A services, then the law will expect it to comply with the legislation and case law applying to a Part A procurement.

Note that throughout this book the assumption is that procurements of health services will be conducted as if those services fell into Part A.

Where can I find out about upcoming procurements of public sector services?

Most significant procurements[12] will be advertised in the OJEU. This was once a paperback book that was published, printed and distributed six days a week, but is now a published online and updated every working day.

Over one hundred notices are published most days and a rather unscientific survey (i.e. a one-off check of the OJEU at the time of writing) shows 4,443 current notices[13] for contract opportunities in the United Kingdom covering the whole range of supplies and services across the public and utilities sectors.

A small industry has grown up where organisations search the OJEU for opportunities to suit particular prospective bidders. Whether it is worth paying for such services is debatable because the notices can be viewed free of charge at: http://ted.europa.eu[14], a web site that is open to all. There is a

12. i.e. those with a value higher than the thresholds (see below).

13. i.e. notices for which the deadline to respond had not expired.

14. TED stands for Tenders Electronic Daily

registration process, but this is simply to provide access to search features and does not demand proof that the registrant has any particular standing. Other sources include:

- for NHS contract opportunities: *Supply2health* at https://www.supply2health.nhs.uk
- for UK public contracts in general: *Contracts Finder* at https://online.contractsfinder.businesslink.gov.uk

The Regulations require that if a contract opportunity is advertised in the OJEU it must neither be advertised elsewhere before despatch of the notice[15] to the OJEU nor contain more information than appears in the OJEU notice.

In theory any contract opportunity above the qualifying thresholds (see below) that appears on either of the above sites must also appear in the OJEU but policing of the Regulations is not sufficiently robust to guarantee this, particularly as some purchasers may still be using the Part B services opt-out to avoid advertising health opportunities in the OJEU.

For the time being it is safer to trawl all sites for opportunities.

How do I apply to become a bidder?

Normally the bidder's first step in the procurement process is to respond to a Contract Notice with an *expression of interest*.

There is no set form of expression of interest, but the Contract Notice should tell you how to do it. With the increasing use of electronic procurement systems it is often just a matter of registering your name, e-mail address and a few other details on a dedicated procurement website. Once you have registered you will be sent information and procurement documents as they become available.

Information about clarifications, clarification requests, and changes to dates, arrangements or the procedure itself will go to the e-mail address that you give on registration. If you miss this sort of information you put yourself at a disadvantage and could even disqualify yourself. It is risky to change contact details part way through. Electronic systems don't like this and messages might go missing.

15. Note *despatch*, so it is in theory possible for the notice legally to appear elsewhere before it appears in the OJEU.

- ***Make sure that the e-mail address that you provide will stay live for the duration of the procurement process.***
- ***It is reasonable to expect a confirmation of some kind when you express an interest. If you don't see or receive anything that you recognise as such, don't sit and wait – chase up the purchaser and make sure that your interest has been registered. If you have been overlooked you will not be involved in the procurement exercise.***
- ***Expressing an interest commits you to nothing. If you decide not to proceed then just ignore further communications and you should drop off the list automatically.***

What is a procurement hub?

A procurement hub (or collaborative procurement hub) is a public sector organisation that aims to provide procurement services for a group of public sector organisations and is usually owned collaboratively by them. Some hubs are dedicated to the NHS; others cover a broader range of the public sector. The premise is that combined buying power and specialist procurement expertise can deliver a better deal for the customer[16].

Increasingly the bidder's route of communication will be via one of these procurement hubs rather than directly with the purchaser. The intermediation of procurement 'specialists' is not always entirely helpful, however, and can cause delays or worse still misunderstandings.

A particular weakness of this intermediation for both purchaser and bidder is that each procurement specialist handles several procurements and if that person is not available (perhaps away from the office tending to another procurement exercise) then communication between purchaser and bidders comes to a temporary halt.

The role of the hub's specialist in handling clarification questions can be

16. In theory good for bulk-buying of bandages, but not necessarily for a professional service regulated by legislation or contracts where the expertise lies with specialists within the purchaser organisation. Clearly a one-off saving can be made by aggregating buying power thus funding the procurement hub with its overheads of premises, employees, directors, etc but once the bulk discounts have been achieved what incentive is there for the customers to continue funding the hub? And if the procurement hub has negotiated the best possible discount this year, how can it expect to beat suppliers down even further next year? These are interesting questions, made more interesting by the fluid nature of these constantly changing organisations, but not for further consideration here.

a little uncertain. Most questions will be about the requirement itself and so be for the purchaser to answer; others will concern procedural or legal aspects of the procurement and will be for the specialist to answer[17]; but many fall between[18].

The balance of responsibility depends very much on the nature of the working agreement between the purchaser and the procurement hub, to the extent that in some cases the procurement hub acts simply as a message handling service.

- ***Be aware that the staff at the procurement hub and the staff at the purchaser have different views and priorities which may have an effect on the flow of information or even on the validity of the answers provided.***
- ***Be careful about subverting the stipulated information pathway by, say, communicating directly with the purchaser. If the purchaser (even innocently) replies to you alone you may be giving other bidders grounds for challenging the procurement.***

The context of procurement

Imagine yourself contemplating whether you should throw your hat into the ring and bid for a contract for the supply of public services. If you have kept up with current affairs over the last few years you will have heard or read of a fair number of high profile public procurement projects that have gone badly wrong. Defence-related procurements feature prominently among them, and admittedly these are special cases, but the NHS and other parts of the public services have had their share as well.

But the contract that you are contemplating is a relatively modest affair; it couldn't happen to the procurement you are thinking about, could it? Well

17. Except that the lawyers may be working directly for the purchaser and may take a different view of the law to the hub's specialist, thus complicating matters even more.

18. The author was called in to advise on a procurement of services that was already under way. Two forms of contract applied to the services (call them type A and type B). The difference between the contracts was minimal, but they applied to different classes of suppliers. There was considerable overlap, but nevertheless for all potential bidders to be able to bid the option of using either contract type had to be allowed. Between the service experts and the procurement experts this fact was lost and the procurement experts had placed a notice that mentioned contract type A only. Lawyers advised that this was inequitable as it excluded suppliers who could only sign contract type A. On legal advice, the procurement was aborted and started again, this time making it clear that either contract type A or contract type B could be used.

probably not, at least in the sense that it is unlikely to hit the headlines with winner and purchasing organisation being dragged into disrepute. Even so most public procurements are flawed to a greater or lesser degree and sometimes those flaws can have serious consequences for some or all of the bidders.

There is no shortage of advice on how to run a procurement under the Regulations, so why do things go awry? The simple answer is that the process is run by human beings and human beings are fallible creatures, but there are also more specific reasons that stem from the environment in which most purchasers operate. It is helpful for the prospective bidder to understand them.

- **Scope of the Regulations** – obeying the procedures set out in the Regulations is a necessary but not sufficient requirement for a good procurement. The Regulations are silent on many of the finer aspects of the procedures and the purchaser is left to design the details with only the principles of the Regulations for guidance.

  Some aspects of procedure are clearly defined in the Regulations in black and white, for example the thirty-seven day period between publishing the notice in the OJEU and *the last date for the receipt by [the purchaser] of requests to be selected to tender*[19]. On the other hand equitable treatment of bidders is a matter of judgement, and that judgement can be obscured by the purchaser's zeal in following the defined procedures.

- **Shortage of experience** – the need to procure a service does not come around frequently in any one organisation, so those who gained appropriate experience last time are likely to have moved on. Often the same lessons must be learned all over again.

- **Skills gap** – many procurements are the responsibility of people who know little of the practice of public procurement, so they seek advice from procurement experts. Unsurprisingly the procurement experts don't know much about the technical aspects of what is

19. Regulation 16(3) of the Public Contracts Regulations 2006. Some might argue with black and white – the clock actually starts when the notice is despatched not when published; and 'days' means calendar days, not working days, which makes for difficulties with, for example, Microsoft Project where the standard calendar recognises weekends as days off; and is the date of despatch day 0 or day 1?

being procured. This leaves a gap down which all manner of things can fall.

- **Shortage of resource** – the person running the procurement will usually be doing it alongside his or her day job. The same applies to evaluators who must generally cram their marking into the time between meetings or take their work home. Add to this that evaluation is a tedious process and evaluators tend to underestimate the time required and you do not have a recipe for consistency or a high quality end product.

- **Uncertainty about numbers** – In the early stages of a procurement project the purchaser's ability to plan its workload and therefore define with accuracy the project timetable is constrained by the uncertainty about the number of potential bidders. Factors such as the state of the market (e.g. are there other similar procurements in progress elsewhere?), the location of the services, the nature of the requirement (e.g. is it a standard service or is there an element of novelty in it?) or even the perceived attractiveness of the purchaser as a client can mean that the number of potential bidders expressing an interest can vary from a single figures to the low hundreds.

- **Paralysis by (legal) analysis** – above all else purchasers fear challenge by aggrieved suppliers; it matters not whether this is a reasonable fear, it is a fear nonetheless. The result is over-caution with every step in the process being over-analysed and passed to the lawyers (and the advice that comes back frequently takes the form of *on the one hand... but on the other hand... so it's your decision*).

- **The tyranny of deadlines**[20] – it is regrettable but true that some purchasing organisations drag their feet when it comes to setting up a procurement process. There are many reasons: no one has noticed that the end of the current contract is approaching; effort and timescale are underestimated; no one can be found in the organisation

---

20. It is commonly held that the Regulations lengthen the procurement process. There may be many valid grounds for criticising the Regulations, but this is not one of them. In terms of tasks and timescales the Regulations ask nothing more than what any reasonable public sector organisation would do whether the Regulations applied or not.

with the time or the skills, still less the inclination, to run the project; the perceived awfulness of the public sector procurement process has caused heads to be buried in the sand; or even a refusal to accept that the Regulations apply at all[21].

Nevertheless there is usually a conviction, especially among senior management, that time can be 'pulled back' to meet the deadline that has crept up so sneakily. Time is stolen from vulnerable sections of the project plan, such as the initial planning stage (*Get the advert in the OJEU asap. It'll save time*[22]) or from the evaluation stage.

- **Organisational process** – public sector organisations have their own internal processes that must be observed by the procurement project. For instance some organisations will require that significant decisions must be endorsed or agreed[23] by a board or committee that meets on set dates only. Tying in a procurement schedule to these dates can add time to the project.

  Minor holdups to the project cause a set date to be missed and so turn a delay of a few days into a month or more. Worse still interference from higher management keen to accelerate the project can seriously damage its integrity.

21. The author was once invited to discuss the possibility of running a procurement project for a public sector organisation. He explained the procedure and the obligations to equitable treatment, etc. The manager, dynamic and newly arrived from the private sector, became impatient with what he was hearing. The rules restricted his freedom as a decision maker; there must be some way round them. The author replied that there were ways round, but not within the law. Needless to say the author was not engaged. This is a somewhat extreme example of the attitude adopted by purchasers, but in a surprising context. The organisation was an Ofsomething, responsible for ensuring compliance with various rules and principles that of late have come very much to the fore in public debate.
22. Not if you haven't specified the requirement or the procurement methodology first it won't!
23. Such a practice is open to question, for the two major decisions made in a procurement – membership of the short-list and choice of contractor – are not decisions in the sense that one or more persons deliberate on evidence then arrive at a judgement. They are in fact the inevitable outcome of following a process as set out previously (a process that might be described as designing a procurement engine according to the Regulations, turning the handle, then seeing what comes out at the end). What is a committee going to do – revisit the scoring process undertaken by the evaluators? Change a decision on the basis of ... well, what? The time for organisational oversight and approval is when proposals are made for the design of the procurement process, priorities are set, weightings are allocated, methods of combining price and quality scores are proposed. And even this can be disastrous. The author saw a procurement of GP services where the proposed methodology had been passed to higher authority for approval and came back with the weightings of the five sections of the ITT decreed as equal, thus the clinical aspects of the proposal counted for 20% of the marks – the same weighting as the quality of the premises.

- **Ignorance of the Regulations at a high level** – senior politicians often speak of public procurement as if they can make up the law as they go along. They amuse and dismay at the same time.

  In 2010 the government in the shape of Cabinet Office[24] minister Francis Maude announced a plan for public sector workers to set up 'John Lewis-style co-operatives', with the aim of 'liberating' public sector workers and 'introduce[ing] radical shifts in ownership, accountability and financing'. He went on to say that 'every government department and every local council will be expected to put in place a right to provide, with the ultimate decision to go ahead resting with the relevant minister'.

  Unfortunately and apparently unknown to the minister such a policy is contrary to the Regulations. As Professor Peter Kunzlik of the City Law School, City University London wrote[25] 'The plan ... seems to assume that service contracts will be awarded without competition. It is, however, hard to see how that could possibly be lawful under EU law. The public contracts directive (2004/18)[26] requires that contracting authorities "shall treat economic operators equally and non-discriminatorily and shall act in a transparent way"'.

  When in 2013, as part of this initiative, Mr Maude announced with great fanfare the privatisation of the government's Behavioural Insights Team (also known as the nudge unit) it was neither John Lewis-style, nor did it appear to be workers liberating themselves. An EU procurement process was initiated to find a 'partner' for the unit, i.e. more or less a standard outsourcing process where internal staff are taken on by a new contractor (see the section on TUPE below) with the only nod to the co-operative model being that between them staff were to receive 25% of the new organisation's shares.

  How many other procurement strategies are imposed from on high with less publicity, but a similar degree of ignorance?

- **Failure of common sense** – the purchaser's fear of the perceived complexity of the Regulations and of committing transgressions against due process can obscure all other considerations and common sense slips quietly out of the back door.

24. The very department responsible for oversight of public procurement policies!
25. http://www.guardian.co.uk/society/2010/nov/23/lewis-plans-risk-being-oversold
26. i.e. the European directive implemented in the UK as the Public Contracts Regulations 2006.

- **The search for the Right Result** – it is unfortunate but undeniable that some purchasers go into a procurement with preconceptions and one of the most common is that of a Right Result.

  What this means differs from purchaser to purchaser[27]. Many factors come into consideration including fear of the unknown, the need for a 'warm feeling', regard for the opinion of senior management, the memory of previous 'bad' experiences, a wish to avoid suppliers with a bad reputation and, above all, the desire for the decision to be 'safe'. The search for the Right Result is understandable, but it can easily slide into subjectivity and abuse of the procurement process.

What are PQQs and ITTs?

They are Pre-qualification Questionnaires and Invitations to Tender. Crudely put, both are documents containing questions, except that the ITT also has a question about price. In practice this is how many writers of these documents see them as well, but it isn't quite that simple.

Pre-qualification Questionnaire

The PQQ is sent to all prospective bidders who have expressed an interest. It will usually explain the requirement, set out a timetable and explain the process (each to a greater or lesser degree according to the inclination of the purchaser) but as far as the purchaser is concerned the PQQ's main purposes are a) to weed out bidders who are not capable or unsuitable; and b) to establish a hierarchy of suitable bidders so that a short-list can be drawn up[28].

The Regulations effectively mandate several of the questions that must appear in the PQQ. These are mostly about financial matters and will ask about failure to pay your taxes, convictions for bribery, etc.

27. It also differs according to point of view. What is perceived as right for the purchaser may not necessarily be right for the taxpayer or the user of the services.

28. An additional purpose of the PQQ is to establish a few facts about the identity and legal form of the bidder. This is not a trivial issue. The purchaser needs to know who or what the bidding entity is or will be, for if this is uncertain how can the bidder's capability be assessed? Is it a sole trader? Partnership? Company? Charity? What is the address? Does the entity exist or will it only be set up if the bid is successful? This information can be collected in other ways, but collection in the PQQ formalises it.

Add to the questions about your propensity to commit financial crimes the questions about financial standing and there are a lot of questions that are yes/no, pass/fail or involve supplying standard information about your business[29].

Invitation to Tender

You will only receive an ITT if you have been successful at the PQQ stage and so have been short-listed.

The ITT may repeat or even modify some of the procedural information provided in the PQQ (timetable, process, etc) and by this stage you can reasonably expect to see a definitive and detailed statement of the requirement and a draft contract (if you haven't seen this information earlier).

Whereas the majority of questions in the PQQ are to some extent constrained or even dictated by the Regulations, in the ITT the purchaser is free to set its own questions about the nature of your proposed service and how it will be delivered. This is where you tailor your answers to the particular characteristics and requirements of the purchaser.

The ITT also contains that all important question about price. You can be requested to present your price in a number of ways: a simple monthly or annual price for supplying the service; separate prices for each element of the service; volume-related costs; or in even more complex formats. The ITT may sometimes request additional information about the assumptions that underlie your calculations.

What is an electronic procurement system?

An electronic procurement system fulfils a number of functions, some important ones being to maintain an auditable record of communications between purchaser and bidders[30], time-stamping all transactions passing through the system and enabling the electronic submission of bidders' responses to the PQQ and the ITT.

The systems were originally designed for the purchase of goods and so they have the capability of presenting PQQs and ITTs as online questionnaires, where the bidder types answers (or pastes pre-prepared material) into boxes

29. The scope of the questions that can be asked in a PQQ is set out in Part 4 of the Public Contracts Regulations (2006),

30. An audit trail can be maintained using ordinary e-mail, but it does not carry the high security classification of an electronic procurement system, i.e. e-mail messages can go missing, but messages cannot be lost from an electronic procurement system, either deliberately or accidently.

that appear against the questions. A partially completed response can be left and returned to later, and submission only happens when the submit button is (electronically) pressed by the bidder.

It is arguable whether online questions and responses are as suitable for the procurement of services as for the simpler dialogue used in the procurement of goods. The online method does not allow the layout and formatting, either in the question or in the answer, that are so essential to conveying the bidder's full meaning. This may be a satisfactory method of answering a few technical questions about widgets, but it is not a good way of submitting a coherent description of an element of a service.

In their early days these systems were clunky and unforgiving. A limit to the number of characters that could be entered into a box meant that answers were truncated without the bidder being aware and whole responses could be lost through failure of the system or of those operating them.

Data integrity and other aspects of the systems have improved, but, nevertheless if you are faced with an online questionnaire take precautions.

- ***The questionnaire format is particularly poor at displaying the paragraphs of factual and instructional material that are so essential to a bidder's understanding of the requirements, so make sure that you read the document especially carefully.***
- ***Prepare your answers off-line using a word processor with which you are comfortable (but, unless you are confident that the system will reproduce them faithfully, do not use any fancy formatting or special characters) and paste them into the answer boxes.***
- ***Save your pre-prepared response in case you need it again.***
- ***Check on character limits and obey them.***
- ***There should be a facility that allows you to check your response before pressing the submit button. Re-read diligently, checking especially that there is no truncation.***
- ***If the system allows it, download a copy of your submission in case there is any argument later.***

If, however, the purchaser uses the system more sensibly then documents will be written in the conventional way and made available for downloading. Similarly, rather than filling in an online questionnaire, bidders will upload responses as Word or PDF documents.

One important point to note about communication via an electronic procurement system is that to maintain the audit trail all significant communication takes place within the system. The only messages that are sent outside the system are standard-form e-mails to tell a bidder that it has a message. The bidder must then sign on to the system to read the message.

- ***Ensure that the person who receives the e-mails also has access to the electronic procurement system; otherwise there will be delays in dealing with what might be time-critical messages.***

Electronic procurement systems can seem daunting at first, but in essence are not as difficult to use as some mail-order websites.

- ***Nevertheless, ensure that you fully understand how the electronic procurement system operates AND how the purchaser wants you to use it; and***
- ***If it is possible practice using it before you begin serious attempts at writing your submission.***

With some methods of handling bidders' submissions – postal or e-mail for example – exact precision of timing is not possible, but electronic procurement systems are ruthless – when the deadline comes they bring down an electronic barrier that prevents further submission.

On the whole, electronic procurement systems are relatively self-explanatory and easy to use, BUT…

- ***when making a submission via an electronic procurement system, don't leave pressing the submit button until the last minute – that's when things go wrong.***

How can I get more information?

The contract notice or other advertisement will contain an outline of the requirement but often it is neither very informative nor particularly accurate.

Many notices are drawn up in haste and some have to be corrected by re-advertisement thus restarting the procurement clock.

Sometimes a briefing document will be sent to anyone expressing an interest but the most likely place for the requirement to be set out in detail is the PQQ and/or ITT.

- ***Use every means available to gather as much information as possible as early as possible.***

The full details of the service description will be defined in the contract signed by the purchaser and contractor, but a draft contract should be issued early in the process and should address some of the basic requirements. Even these bare bones might have a bearing on your response. For example, the duration of the agreement could be a deciding factor as to whether you take part.

- ***Ensure that you understand the general form and major aspects of the contract as early as possible and certainly before you begin your response to the ITT.***

Many purchasers hold bidder events where they describe some or all of their organisation, their requirement and the process. These tend to be held either soon after the notice is published – open to all comers with the intention, in theory, of assisting potential bidders in deciding whether to enter – or after expressions of interest have closed when only interested bidders are invited (and sometimes at both stages).

During a bidder event the purchaser will invite questions from attendees. Following the bidder event written versions of the questions and answers and any slides used will be made available to all at attendees and any other interested parties unable to attend.

- ***Make sure that the person primarily responsible for responding to the PQQ and ITT attends the bidder event. Written questions and answers cannot reproduce the full tenor of what was said, still less expressions on faces.***
- ***Prepare for the bidder event by studying any documents that you have been sent and by finding out as much as you can about the purchaser.***

But if neither documentation nor bidder event provide you with sufficient information, then your next recourse is to the clarification process.

What is a clarification process?

Procurement runs better if there is a continuing full and open dialogue between purchaser and bidders. In a well-run procurement this is facilitated via a formal clarification process.

The clarification process operates in both directions. Bidders use it to seek information such as a better understanding of the requirement or the precise meaning of a part of a document. Purchasers use it to seek additional information from bidders, to correct or clarify published documents or to provide information about administrative matters.

- ***Use the clarification process to ensure that you have a full understanding of the requirement and of the procedure. Ask questions if you need to and study answers to other bidders' questions.***

Whether or not to ask a question via the clarification process, or at a bidder event, can seem to pose a dilemma – *what's the point? If it helps me it will help everyone else as well. Worse still I might look silly*[31].

- ***Forget about looking silly. If the question is asked as a clarification your name should be withheld anyway and at a bidder event most other bidders will wish that they had had the courage to ask for themselves. Knowledge is always better than ignorance – back yourself to gain more from the answer than your competitors.***

The clarification process must, of course, comply with the three basic principles of equitable treatment, non-discrimination and transparency, and what is more the purchaser must be able to demonstrate that this is so. The general rule is that all questions and all answers (going in whichever direction between purchaser and bidders) must be shared with all bidders[32].

The usual medium of communication is e-mail, sent either directly or indirectly via an electronic procurement system.

- ***It is essential that as a bidder you understand the clarification process. If the purchaser's description is inadequate, then ask a clarification question.***

Any attempt by a bidder to seek information over the telephone or by other informal means ought to elicit the response in the form of *please submit*

31. On the other hand you are unlikely to gain any advantage with purchasers by asking 'clever' questions.

32. The only exchanges that can be withheld are those that are definitely specific to one bidder, but don't expect to get an answer to a question such as 'are my current premises good enough to score top marks in the property section of the evaluation?' (Nevertheless, there's nothing to be lost by trying!)

that question via the formal clarification process. If *you* receive information outside the process then you have a dilemma, especially if you are the sole recipient of the information. If the information gives you an advantage and the other bidders find out they have good grounds for launching a challenge[33].

- ***It is unlikely these days that any purchaser would be so ignorant of the rules as to fail to run a transparent clarification process, but if you suspect otherwise raise your concerns with the purchaser as soon as possible.***

Answers (and other information) must be sent to all bidders, including the questioner, at the same time and have the same content. It is not usual to identify the questioner. The proper form is something like *a bidder has asked the following question.... and the following response is provided ....*

Even where a clarification question is being sent by the purchaser and appears to apply only to a specific bidder care is needed. Take, for example, the situation where one bidder's answer shows that a question can quite reasonably be interpreted in a way not intended by the setter and until that point the ambiguity has not been recognised by the purchaser nor, on the basis of their responses, by any other bidder. At first sight it seems the sensible course is for the purchaser to explain the intended meaning and allow the bidder to resubmit its answer.

In the interests of equitable treatment, however, it is probably safer to allow all bidders a second chance, using a formula such as *some bidders have misunderstood the meaning of question X. The intended meaning is as follows ... Should any bidder wish to resubmit its response to this question then it must do so before [time and date].*

- ***You must be in a position to answer any questions or act on any information that comes through the clarification process immediately. Make sure that:***
    - ***your e-mail address is permanent (at least for the duration of the procurement) and your e-mail service provider is reliable;***
    - ***your e-mails are monitored regularly (at least twice a day, including weekends);***
    - ***your e-mail will not reject procurement-related communications as spam; and***

33. On the other hand it could be the 'wrong' answer untested by exposure to all bidders and could disadvantage you alone.

- ***you continue to monitor e-mails until you are certain that the procurement is over (if, for example, a bidder challenges the process at a late stage e-mails could start flying in all directions).***

What are Selection and Award?

The Regulations make a clear distinction between the PQQ short-listing process (*selection* in EU-speak) and the choice of the winner on the basis of responses to the ITT (*award* in EU-speak).

The simplest way to describe this difference is that the selection process is an evaluation of the bidder – does the bidder have the capability and capacity to provide the service – whereas the award process is an evaluation of the bid – does the proposed service meet the requirements of the purchaser[34] and does it offer best value for money?

It follows that the PQQ shouldn't ask how you will provide the service and the ITT shouldn't ask whether you have the ability to provide the service. Unfortunately, as is shown by the number of legal actions that have hinged on this point, distinguishing between questions that assess the capability of the bidder and those that assess the worth of the bid is not always easy.

A rather crude example is: *please state where you have provided or provide similar services to those required here*. This question should not appear in the ITT because it is a clear attempt to reassess capability, however if the question then went on to say: *and explain how you will transfer the lessons learned from those services to the services defined here*, then the distinction is not so clear. It is in these grey areas that lawyers earn their fees.

- ***If you believe that a question in the ITT is an attempt to reassess your capability as a bidder rather than to assess the quality of your bid, the best time to challenge is as soon as you read the question. Put the issue directly to the purchaser. At worst although your protest might be dismissed at the time you have put down a marker for later.***
- ***If the purchaser tells you that you have failed at the ITT stage because of your lack of experience then you might have a case for challenging the decision.***

34. Or even by how much does it exceed the requirements? We discuss acceptability or rather adequacy elsewhere in this book.

Is there a continuum from PQQ to ITT?

Some bidders and even some purchasers are under the misapprehension that there is continuity from PQQ to ITT. In the sense that a bidder must pass the PQQ stage before moving to the ITT stage, this is true, but only in that sense. As is explained above, the PQQ and the ITT have distinctly different purposes.

In a properly ordered procurement the results of the PQQ evaluation have no place in the decision on who gets the contract, nevertheless bidders can be anxious on this matter and ask questions such as *at the ITT stage will you be taking into account anything I said in my PQQ response?*

- ***It is to be hoped that the answer to such a question would be a firm 'no', but if you have any suspicions that the purchaser will be taking another look at the PQQ responses when it evaluates the tenders then you need to find out what is going on and, if necessary, object immediately.***

Having said that, an overlap between the PQQ response and the tender is still possible. For example, the PQQ will seek information on your experience in the relevant field of expertise. It is possible, especially if such experience is scarce in the market as a whole, to be short-listed despite citing little in the way of such experience.

If you then go on to say in your tender something like *the quality of our service will be informed by our extensive experience in delivering this type of service* you are asking for a clarification question and a disgruntled evaluator or worse the scoring of the whole of your tender being prejudiced (rightly, it might be argued) on the grounds that where it can be checked you have been economical with the truth.

- ***Ensure that nothing that you say in your tender contradicts what you said in your PQQ response.***

Are purchasers obliged to tell you their budgetary limit or price ceiling?

There is no good reason why bidders shouldn't be told about budgetary limits, nevertheless purchasers often don't like to because they fear that bidders will bid up to the limit. The response to this is not if they have any sense they won't – that's what competitive tendering is all about.

Unfortunately, some purchasers don't fully trust the competitive process. They cite commercial confidentiality and keep their budgetary limits secret. And to be realistic it is in the nature of things that purchasers don't always know their budgetary limit.

Of course, if a bidder can be excluded for exceeding a price ceiling then the principle of transparency demands that the limit must be revealed. Unfortunately, squeamishness about revealing costs means that sometimes limits are withheld even in these circumstances[35].

- ***Do your best to find out whether there is a price ceiling, and if so, its value. If it turns out that the limit is set unreasonably low and no conscientious bidder would have a hope of getting under it, then you might be able to reclaim any money wasted so far on your bid[36].***
- ***Make sure that you know whether exceeding a price ceiling automatically excludes a bidder[37] (and if it does, don't exceed it or don't bid!)***

Who can see my bid?

It can come as a surprise to bidders that information submitted in the course of a public procurement process is subject to publication under the Freedom of Information Act (FOIA). And this means, with some minor exceptions, the whole of the bid including the tender, the PQQ response and any documents that have been submitted as annexes or appendices to either the PQQ or the ITT.

- ***Don't enter a bidding process unless you are prepared for the entirety of your bid to enter the public domain.***

35. This can lead purchasers into all sorts of problems when they discover that they can't afford the bid that comes out top (it has happened). Unfortunately, proving that an evaluation has been 'revisited' for these reasons is not easy.
36. Or rather you might have a cause for action, but would it be worth the effort and legal costs for a relatively low return? Better to find out the facts before you commit to much time and effort.
37. Regrettably, you might find that there is reluctance to provide a clear answer on this point, especially the automatic exclusion aspect. Purchasers like to keep their options open, especially if they haven't clarified their evaluation process sufficiently. You may have to insist on an answer using the implied threat that failure to reveal a limit could be grounds for challenge.

Any requests under FOIA for information during the course of a procurement would rightly be rejected on the grounds of commercial confidentiality – it would be a nonsense if one bidder could apply to see its competitors' documents before the purchaser had reached its decision. But it is not unusual for purchasers to receive requests for copies of bids, especially winning bids, after the decision has been reached. Usually these come either from unsuccessful bidders who are considering a challenge to the result or from organisations seeking information to assist in other bids[38].

Legal opinion is that the only information that can be withheld under an FOIA request is personal data (usually dealt with by redacting names and other means of identification) and commercially confidential data. Interpretations of what is commercially confidential vary, but purchasers are reluctant to admit to what they have paid for a contract so they use commercial confidentiality as justification for withholding the bid prices. It is unlikely therefore, although by no means impossible, that the price of your bid will be revealed, although if you win the contract the price will come out sooner or later[39].

- ***Do not place any reliance on a purchaser allowing you to specify which parts of your submission should not be revealed under FOIA. You do not have a veto. It is the purchaser who is answerable under law and the Information Commissioner is the final arbiter of what must be released.***

Sometimes bidders are asked to submit copies of their protocols and procedures as part of their tender. These are likely to have been painstakingly developed over the years and bidders argue that they contain their business secrets so deserve to remain confidential. The law disagrees however and there is no protection for such documents save the law of copyright (for what that is worth in these circumstances!).

Despite their obligations under the FOIA there is a perhaps understandable reluctance on the part of purchasers to release information. Many reasons are cited (informally and orally, of course – anything in writing is subject to release under FOIA) often expressing the highest of motives such as

38. The thinking goes that an answer that receives high marks in one procurement will score well in another. This is not necessarily a safe assumption – evaluators will definitely and evaluation criteria will probably be different.

39. The Information Commissioner seems to take the view that time erodes the confidentiality of the contract price, so by the time it is revealed it is unlikely that anyone will be interested.

respect for the privacy of bidders or the danger of putting off bidders from competing in future procurements.

In practice what is released under FOIA depends first upon the stance of the purchaser, then the tenacity of the requestor and finally[40] on how the Information Commissioner interprets the law.

- ***If the purchaser is inclined to resist the release of information in response to an FOIA request then the requestor is faced with a tedious and time consuming appeal process. This might be enough to put off some requestors, but don't rely on it.***

What if I miss something from a response?

You may have submitted your response well before the deadline then to your horror realise that something has been missed out or you have given a wrong answer. It's unlikely that any purchaser would prevent an additional submission of missing information before the deadline, but attitudes to 'corrections' might vary – how many attempts does a bidder need to get it right?

- ***If you realise that you have missed something from your response after you have submitted it, but before the deadline has passed, send in the missing information with an explanation. Make sure that you get an acknowledgement of receipt.***
- ***If you want to amend your response before the deadline think carefully about how you do it. What, if anything, do the instructions to bidders say? Pre-deadline amendment is unlikely to be specifically forbidden, but check with the purchaser that it is allowed, implying that you are seeking equitable treatment.***

The first substantive action of a purchaser after the deadline will be to check whether each bid is complete. What the purchaser does if it finds anything missing depends on circumstances. Fear of challenge, a wish to keep as many players as possible in the game, a desire to be reasonable: any of these can prompt the purchaser to ask a bidder to submit missing information.

Whether the purchaser is sensible to take this approach is debatable. Consider, for example, a supporting document that proves to be unreadable. The most likely explanation is that the fault lies with the bidder, but there

40. If, that is, the requestor appeals to the Information Commissioner and then *finally* can be many months after the original request to the purchaser.

is always a small chance that the fault may have been introduced during transmission or at the purchaser's end.

The IT department could be called in to conduct an investigation and determine where in the chain of transmission responsibility lies, but this would take up time and might not be conclusive. The quickest and most reasonable solution is to inform the bidder and request resubmission.

But this has set a precedent that can be stretched further. Now every other omission and obvious mistake must be considered for a second chance. What about a red flag question that has been missed? After all, the instructions were quite clear, so missing an answer in the knowledge that this would mean instant exclusion must be a genuine and honest mistake, must it not?

And what about the submission deadline itself? It would be harsh to exclude a bidder who misses the deadline by a few minutes, especially when using an electronic procurement system which can confuse bidders and even go wrong; but what of a delay of hours or even days?

- ***If you realise that you have missed something after the submission deadline has passed then it is still worth submitting the information with an explanation for the delay.***
- ***There may be circumstances – to register the need for due process with the purchaser, perhaps, or where you wish to assess your chances of doing the same – in which it is a sensible precaution to ask the purchaser whether there have been any late submissions, additions or corrections from other bidders.***
- ***Notwithstanding all of the above, provided that every bidder is treated equitably, the purchaser can refuse to accept material that has been submitted after the deadline so don't bank on the purchaser checking the completeness of your submission or allowing you to make a late amendment or addition.***

Can I negotiate in a procurement process?

The EU deprecates negotiation because it 'distorts competition'. It is therefore forbidden in all but the strictly circumscribed Negotiated procedure.

Negotiation is in essence any discussion that impacts on the price or changes the scope of the contract, which is the obverse of changing the price. For example *if you could drop your price by £10k then your bid would have a much better chance* or *what if we removed the obligation to paint the fence every year*[41]?

The Regulations demand that all cards are on the table before any decision is made. The contract signed by the successful bidder must be substantially the same draft contract and be based on the service specification issued to all bidders with or before the ITT. The price committed to must be that submitted by the successful bidder and must comply with the price schedule defined in the ITT.

Nevertheless, there is always the temptation for bidders and purchasers alike to fall into a conversation that can look like negotiation. This is understandable, especially when the purchaser is moving into what is for it a new area, such as outsourcing some of its activities for the first time.

The most accessible source of information on how to set up and run the services might well be the potential providers themselves. It is a short path from seeking information to asking a supplier *what can you do for us*? and then 'refining' the service specification to fit the best answers (or what the purchaser perceives to be the best answers).

This version of negotiation became quite common when services were first brought under the EU procurement umbrella. This is why the EU eventually devised and brought into law the competitive dialogue procedure to formalise an iterative process of seeking information whilst forbidding negotiation.

Before the contract is signed there will be dialogue between purchaser and successful bidder, but it should be restricted to matters of clarification and fact such as the names of first points of contact.

- ***If you are lucky enough to be selected as the winning bidder don't then expect to turn up at a meeting accompanied by your lawyer bearing a list of 'a few points to be settled before my client signs the contract'. Any sensible purchaser will point you towards the exit*[42].**

41. Discussing the price separately with each supplier is clearly negotiation. Whether or not a simultaneous announcement to all bidders that all prices are too high would fall foul of the Regulations is a subject for debate. Removing the obligation to paint the fence, however, as well as being negotiation is changing the scope of the contract and would also fall foul of the Regulations for the reason that potential bidders who had no painting department might have decided not to bid for that very reason.
42. When this happened in the author's presence he gave the bidder a firm talking to and neither the exit, nor the lawyer for that matter, were needed.

The absolute prohibition of negotiation is one of the primary reasons why communications between purchasers and bidders should as far as possible be limited to writing and a scrupulous audit trail must be maintained

- ***Evidence of negotiation between purchaser and (a) bidder/s would be grounds for challenging the procurement. But where does dialogue end and negotiation begin?***

Elephant traps

Purchasers don't deliberately dig elephant traps; more often than not they are dug by the bidder and sometimes they prove fatal.

Preparing a response to a PQQ or an ITT is an unfamiliar and stressful process where the obvious can be overlooked. The bidder is at greatest danger at the PQQ stage where the purchaser is faced with the daunting task of reducing, say, sixty bidders down to a short-list of six or so.

This is grindingly boring work where sympathy is at a premium. Even the most saintly of evaluators can be forgiven for leaping on a silly mistake made by a bidder if it means immediate exclusion and thus one less submission to mark.

Consider the production of financial information at the PQQ stage. A corporate entity will generally be required to produce three years' audited accounts, but for an individual or small partnership this can mean revealing information from a private bank account or calculations used for tax purposes.

- ***Don't respond by saying 'contact my accountant'. It's your responsibility to produce the information and if you don't the purchaser is perfectly entitled to reject your bid out of hand.***
- ***If you don't have an accountant make sure that any financial information is provided in full and is presented tidily. Hand written calculations do not impress!***
- ***If you can't provide the required information in full ask the purchaser if what you do have will suffice.***

Often bidders will ask for financial projections or business plans to support the bid price, i.e. to show that you can afford to deliver the required services on the basis of the projected revenue[43].

43. It is an interesting debate as to whether this question is about the bidder or the bid, i.e. is a PQQ or an ITT question.

- ***Don't produce financial projections that show that you will operate at a loss! If so then why are you bidding[44]?***

Some purchasers will set out precise requirements about, say, the geographical location at which services must be delivered and underline this by assigning a red flag to the question.

- ***If you are answering a red flag question make sure that you meet the requirements. If the requirement is geographical, for example, don't be afraid to consult a map!***

Frequently price contributes 30% of the total score in the ITT evaluation, so if you can't achieve a reasonable score on price you are unlikely to win the bid, however high your quality score.

The ways of calculating the price score are many and varied, but consider a method where a) there is a stated price ceiling; b) zero price points are awarded to a bid at the price ceiling; c) 30 price points are awarded for the lowest price; and d) intermediate prices are awarded price points pro-rata.

There are easy points to be won by pitching the bid at a competitive price somewhere below the ceiling, but nevertheless some bidders will throw away the whole 30% by pricing at the ceiling. And you are unlikely to win a procurement if you throw away 30% of the available points[45].

- ***If you have some financial flexibility, study the scoring mechanism before setting your price.***

Past performance

There ought to be a better way of awarding a contract, especially for a service, than asking bidders a series of questions and taking the answers on trust. Common sense suggests that past performance is a very good indicator, so why not ask a bidder's customers how it has performed previously?

Some of the problems with such an approach are apparent, many of them related to equitable treatment: how do you obtain an objective measure of past performance? What if not all suppliers have relevant experience? What is relevant experience – how similar must it be? How do you rate a bidder

44. This happened. The evaluators knew that: a) it was a strong bidder; b) a loss was in truth extremely unlikely; and c) that in attempting to devise a business plan himself the bidder had gone well beyond the limits of his capability. The bid was rejected.

45. This has happened in a procurement run by the author and it wasn't just the one bidder that shot itself in the foot.

with middling past performance against one with no record, but who makes ambitious promises? Whose experience are you evaluating - that of a parent company; of a member of a consortium; of a major shareholder in a joint venture? But regardless of whether these problems can be overcome, the law severely restricts the degree to which past performance can be used in procuring a service supplier[46].

The problem is addressed in a UK Government Procurement Policy Note[47] a reading of which shows how difficult it is. For a start the policy applies only to:

procuring goods and/or services in respect of information and communications technology, facilities management or business processing outsourcing with a total anticipated contract value of £20 million or greater.

The rigour of the test does not necessarily inspire the taxpayer with confidence:

Departmental Bodies should ask for specified information (which will include certificates of performance) about past performance in the last 3 years. They should then satisfy themselves:

a) that the principal contracts of those who would provide the goods and/or services have been satisfactorily performed in accordance with their terms; or

b) where there is evidence that this has not occurred in any case, that the reasons for any such failure will not recur if that bidder were to be awarded the relevant contract.

Given that a decision to exclude could invite a legal challenge it would be a brave procurement officer who declared insufficient a promise that the bidder would behave better in future[48]. Add to that the very specificity of the test and the fact that it applies only to high value procurements, then it seems that exclusion of a bidder for poor past performance is, except in very special and limited circumstances, most unlikely.

46. There is little doubt that some egregious errors in public procurements would have been avoided in this way. The reader, as a taxpayer, is at liberty to decide how far these legal niceties overlap the realm of common sense.

47. Procurement Policy Note – Taking Account of Bidder's Past Performance Action Note 09/12 08 November 2012 available at: http://procurement.cabinetoffice.gov.uk/sites/default/files/files/GP_content/Public_procurement_policy

48. This is, of course, the opinion of the author of this book. The authors of the paper appear confident that a properly constituted committee backed up by legal advice could indeed safely identify bidders who offered less than convincing undertakings.

Where consideration of past performance is feasible, it is as a characteristic of the bidder not the bid, so it is a matter for the selection (PQQ) process. If a bidder passes the test and is shortlisted, unless there is a change in the bidder's circumstances later in the procurement process, past performance ceases to matter (or rather should do so if the procurement is properly conducted).

- ***If you suspect that you have been excluded from a short-list for reasons of past performance, then you must ask for an immediate explanation of the decision and consider whether it justifies making a legal challenge.***
- ***Provided that your (relevant) circumstances have not changed any suggestion that you have been marked down or excluded at the award (ITT) stage for past performance must be clarified and if admitted would possibly be grounds for challenge.***
- ***Do not be complacent if you are up against competition that, in your view, has a bad track record – the purchaser has little leeway for excluding them.***

How does evaluation work?

The end product of evaluating a PQQ response or a tender is a number. At the PQQ stage this number is used in selecting the short-list. At the ITT stage it is combined in some mystical way with the price, and perhaps a score for the presentation, to indicate the most economically advantageous tender.

The Regulations say nothing about how these numbers should be arrived at and each purchaser must devise its own way of doing things, but the process usually goes something like this:

- each question[49] is allocated a numerical weighting representing its importance;
- answers are scored on a scale of, say, 0 - 5 according to previously defined scoring guidance or criteria;
- the score for an answer is multiplied by the weight of the question; and
- the weighted scores are added to give the total score.

Of course there will be some questions that go to the heart of the matter, i.e. get the answer wrong and you are unacceptable as a contractor however

49. Often, for simplicity, all questions in a section bear the same weight.

good the remainder of your answers. These are (or should be, if the purchaser knows what it is doing) red flag questions[50]. The process of evaluation will be similar for PQQ responses and tenders, although there is likely to be a higher proportion of yes/no questions in a PQQ and in the ITT there is the all important question on price to be evaluated as well (of which more later).

How do evaluators work?

Evaluators are usually members of the purchaser's staff[51], although in some cases experts may be brought in from elsewhere. Evaluators are chosen for their knowledge and expertise[52] in aspects of the purchaser's requirement and may have been involved in setting the questions.

Usually the questions are split into groups having a common theme and each group is allocated to a particular evaluator or evaluators. The Regulations say nothing about how evaluators should work, but best practice[53] seems to be that each answer is marked independently by two evaluators. If their scores differ they then attempt to come to an agreement; if they can't agree they then turn to a third expert who acts as a moderator.

Best practice also says that evaluators should make their decisions on the basis of the evaluation criteria or other guidance and record their reasons for allocating the score to each answer. These records form the basis for information given to unsuccessful bidders in the Alcatel letter (see below).

Unfortunately best practice does not always apply. It is not easy for a project manager to insist that evaluators follow the rules. The project manager is usually beholden to the evaluators for, in effect, volunteering their time and grateful that they have stepped forward to help out. And by its very nature evaluation is an activity usually carried out in private.

50. The proper use of a red flag question is to define a mandatory requirement and exclude bidders who do not propose to meet it. So, for example, if the red flag question is 'will all treatment will be undertaken by appropriately qualified personnel?' and you answer 'no', then your bid will rightly be rejected without further consideration

51. The recruitment of evaluators is one of the most taxing aspects of running a procurement process because they are being asked to take on a substantial, but undefined amount of work (who knows how many bidders there will be?) on top of their day jobs. Added to that they must be trained in how the process works and in how to conduct themselves with regard to declarations of interest, confidentiality, recording scores and opinions, etc.

52. But given the frequent difficulty of recruiting evaluators, some of the expertise may have been acquired in short order.

53. This is as much to protect the purchaser in the event of a challenge so that it can be shown that a robust evaluation process was used (whether it worked properly is another matter).

Will something said in one answer be taken into account in another?
Purchasers adopt different policies as to whether answers stand alone. In some instances evaluators are forbidden to follow cross-references, in others it is permitted. Regrettably there is a third case where the policy has been given no prior consideration and anything said anywhere in submission, cross-referenced or not, may or may not be taken into account.

- ***If there is no statement in the PQQ/ITT to the effect that each answer stands alone, then ask for clarification so that you (and the purchaser) understand the situation.***
- ***Be aware that any one evaluator may only be allocated a few questions. Repetition of information may be tedious, but it is better than running the risk of information being missed.***
- ***Unless you are quite certain that it is allowed (and even then think carefully about doing it – the evaluator may not be inclined to look) don't refer the evaluator to something you said in another question.***
- ***Despite the above and even if the purchaser practices strict compartmentalisation between answers, remember that evaluators are human and a bad impression made in one answer can influence the evaluation of other answers.***

What are evaluation criteria? Can I see them?
The Regulations require that purchasers reveal their evaluation criteria and the weightings given to them, and courts seem to be supporting the argument that the principle of transparency requires that sub-criteria should also be revealed. This means that criteria and sub-criteria and weightings should be set out in the PQQ, ITT or related documents[54].

The problem is that, despite there being a substantial degree of commonality in the principles of evaluating tenders[55], the law does not have a clear view on what constitutes evaluation criteria and sub-criteria. A court has held, for example, that a statement that price will count for 35% and quality for 65% of the final score are the evaluation criteria[56], thus satisfying the requirements of the Regulations.

54. Certainly with or before the publication of the PQQ or ITT to which they relate.
55. Even so more or less the same wheel is invented over and over again.
56. It was in J Varney & Sons Waste Management Ltd v Hertfordshire Council [2011] EWCA Civ 708. But shouldn't it be is *the evaluation criterion*?

Yet in another case[57] the purchaser argued that sub-criteria are part of the methodology and therefore do not need to be revealed, only for the court to hold that even if that is so transparency demands that the methodology too, and therefore the things called sub-criteria, must be revealed.

It is, frankly, difficult to understand why the law struggles to define what constitutes criteria and sub-criteria. Consider the three elements needed to define an evaluation process:

- instructions to evaluators such as how the answers are allocated between them, how to record results, confidentiality, due dates for results to be submitted etc.;
- an overview of the evaluation process that explains how the overall score for each response is arrived at, covering such things as the weightings given to each question, how the scores are calculated and how to do the sums; and
- guidance to evaluators on scoring, i.e. the objective standards against which an answer is measured. The form of this guidance will depend to some extent on the nature of the question, but it should tell the evaluator what makes a bad answer, a good answer, an excellent answer, etc and therefore what score the question should be awarded.

The first element is of little interest to bidders as it can have little or no impact on the result. The second – which this author calls the evaluation methodology, but the law might call anything including evaluation criteria – and the third – which this author calls the evaluation criteria, but the law may think of as sub-criteria – most definitely are.

Whatever terms are used, and despite some strange legal opinions, it is difficult to argue other than that the principle of transparency requires the second and third elements to be revealed[58] (and remember the law is ever moving in favour of ever greater transparency).

It would be an unusual PQQ or ITT that did not set out the mechanism for arriving at a decision, but, despite, or perhaps because of the various legal precedents, revealing evaluation criteria is a different matter. The problem

57. Sorry, another legal reference: Lettings International Ltd v London Borough of Newham [2008] EWHC 1583.

58. And advice from central government has confirmed this. The Office of Government Commerce has been abolished and unfortunately its definitive advice on procurement seems to have disappeared with it, but that advice was clear about the need to reveal as much information as possible about evaluation guidance and the evaluation process.

is that with neither unambiguous definition of the terms nor guidance on the depth of detail required[59] there is plenty of room for sloppiness on the part of purchasers, who might offer excuses including:

- drawing up evaluation criteria is a high-order skill (a higher-order skill than setting a question) that requires time and effort;
- publishing the evaluation criteria in full is as good as handing out the answers with the exam papers; and
- the project cannot be held up whilst the finer details of evaluation criteria and methodologies are worked out, so there is little detail to be explained in the procurement documents.

So it is not surprising that many purchasers are happy to rely on the 'expertise' of the evaluator who will, of course, know instinctively the difference between an excellent answer and one that is only good[60]. A consequent advantage, for the purchaser that is, of the expertise approach is that there is little or nothing in the way of evaluation criteria to be revealed.

Even when purchasers draw up question-specific evaluation guidance it can be flawed or partial[61]. For example it is not unknown for evaluation criteria to direct evaluators to look for factors that have no place in a rational answer to the question as posed[62] and which would more reasonably be expected to occur in the answer to another question.

The greatest danger to bidders, however, lies in the use of secret or

59. Does, for example, guidance that says scores should be awarded on the basis of 5 for excellent, 4 for *very good* down to 0 for *no relevant content* provide sufficient detail? In the author's opinion no, because it does not provide an objective standard against which an answer can be measured. Nevertheless it is often all there is in the way of evaluation criteria.

60. Another stratagem is for a purchaser to claim that in a multipart question the sub-questions were in themselves the evaluation criteria. Such a claim has been made with the backing of lawyers, but unfortunately was never tested in a tribunal.

61. By a strange coincidence the author was writing this at the same time as the news was breaking about the west-coast main line rail franchising debacle.

62. In fact the author has seen evaluation criteria that expected information in the answer to question 1 that no rational being would consider had any part there, especially as that information was specifically asked for by question 5! This is bizarre, but not funny, because according to these perverse rules an answer that did not contain the unrequested and inappropriate information would have scored at the most 2 out of 5 points. This inappropriate positioning of information was repeated several times across the evaluation scheme, but nevertheless the purchaser got away with it because the rationality of the criteria was never subjected to an independent legal test.

undisclosed evaluation criteria[63], i.e. when the purchaser relies on the argument that criteria are really guidance forming part of the general instructions to evaluators so why should they be revealed?

None of this can be of much comfort to any bidder who cannot afford specialist legal advice in support of the bid, but it is to be hoped that knowing what should be there, but might not be is better than ignorance.

- ***If no criteria are revealed, ask if any exist, especially whether there is any guidance to evaluators that has not been published – even if the reply is partial or evasive you may be building the basis of a challenge.***
- ***If there are evaluation criteria understand them and build your answers around them.***
- ***Make sure that you address all aspects of the question, especially if it is a multipart question, and all points asked for in any evaluation criteria.***
- ***If you fail in your bid try to check whether your answers were properly scored against the published evaluation criteria.***
- ***If you fail and are feeling particularly bloody-minded[64] ask whether there was any unpublished evaluation guidance and back up the enquiry if necessary with a freedom of information request.***

How does short-listing work?

The Regulations describe (but not all that clearly) short-listing[65] as a two stage process: first exclusion of suppliers who are not up to the mark, then, if there are too many left, selection of some them to make up a short-list.

The first stage is described in Regulation 16(7)[66] and, in paraphrase,

63. And it was in secret evaluation criteria, eventually and reluctantly revealed, that the author saw the 'guidance' referred to in a previous footnote where information was expected in an answer to question 1, etc…

64. Tight timescales mean that it is unlikely that you would be able to launch a challenge if you did eventually receive information showing that the process had been flawed, so bloody-mindedness is a necessary requirement for doing this!

65. Nowhere in the Regulations is the term *short-list* used. It is *selection of the economic operators* [Euro-speak for supplier] *to be invited to tender* (Regulation 16(8)). Some authorities hold that the explanation for the rickety nature of the rules for selection is that in much of the EU the market is immature. The problem for purchasers, therefore, is not enough bidders rather than too many. This seems a somewhat lame excuse for failing to describe a clear approach to short-listing.

66. Regulation 16(7) says:

The contracting authority…may exclude an economic operator…only if the economic operator—

(a) may be treated as ineligible to tender on a ground specified in regulation 23 [which sets out all sorts

bidders may be excluded if they:

- have a history of dubious or criminal economic activity;
- lack the financial capability to undertake the work; or
- do not have adequate technical or professional ability.

The first test is objective. It is essentially a series of questions that the bidder is expected to answer truthfully and if an answer is wrong the bidder is rejected. In practice it is rare for a bidder to fail the first test.

The second and third tests are to a degree subjective – what is adequate financial capability or technical ability, especially in the current economic climate?[67] Regulation 16(12) says that if these tests are to be applied the requirements must be *related to and proportionate to the subject matter of the contract*[68]. This is helpful to bidders in that it should discourage bias against smaller bidders, but still leaves room for a lot of subjectivity on the part of the purchaser.

Generally, the number of bidders who pass these tests is greater than it is practical to take through to the ITT stage. The Regulations[69] recognise this[70], but apart from saying that the selection (i.e. short-listing) should be done using

of economic crimes including corruption, bribery, fraud and other heinous offences]; *or*
(b) fails to satisfy the minimum standards required of economic operators by the contracting authority of—
(i) economic and financial standing [regulation 24 specifies the financial information that may be asked for]; *or*
(ii) technical or professional ability [regulation 25 specifies a wide range of information that may be asked for to assess the prospective bidder's technical and professional ability].

67. Which has the best *financial and economic standing*: a multinational that is losing millions every year; a small business that is well in profit, but has shown no appreciable growth for the last three years or a new start-up with finance, but no financial history to present? And on the topic of *technical or professional ability* consider the initial privatisation of British Rail. It would surely have been quite reasonable (sensible?) to set as a minimum standard that potential bidders for franchises should have had previous experience of operating rail services. So why aren't our railways now run by ex-steam enthusiasts from the Bluebell Line and the Severn Valley Railway?

68. Regulation 16(12) also says that exclusion is dependent on *those minimum levels* [being] *specified in the contract notice,* but is a rare contract notice indeed that specifies any such levels.

69. Regulation 16(9) says:
Where there is a sufficient number of economic operators suitable to be selected to be invited to tender, the contracting authority may limit the number of economic operators which it intends to invite to tender provided that the contract notice specifies—
(a) the objective and non-discriminatory criteria to be applied in order to limit the number of economic operators in accordance with this paragraph; and
(b) the minimum number of economic operators, which shall be not less than 5, which the contracting authority intends to invite to tender and, where appropriate, the maximum number.

70. This is sensible. Bidders don't want to waste time and money on a long-shot and the purchasers don't want to be over-burdened with work.

objective and non-discriminatory criteria no more help is offered. A lottery has been held to be objective and non-discriminatory, but few purchasers would use one because of the desire to have what are perceived as the 'best' bidders on the short-list. What usually happens goes something like this:

1. The PQQ will have sections including financial history, financial and economic standing, and technical and professional ability, and the (slightly peripheral) matters of policies covering health and safety, equal opportunities, staff development and environment[71] . The section on technical ability will include questions about experience of similar projects.
2. The vast majority of bidders will skip lightly over the hurdle of dubious financial history.
3. Purchasers will dither about financial and economic standing because it is difficult for reasons already discussed and finance is difficult territory anyway. Whether or not significant numbers of bidders fail at this stage can depend on the attitude and competence of the evaluators and this test is not always done well[72].
4. Strictly speaking according to the Regulations, the purchaser should now assess the bidder's technical and professional ability as pass or fail. The assumption is, however, that thinning out will need to take place, so as answers in this section are: a) capable of being judged on a sliding scale; and b) have a fairly direct relevance to the purchaser's requirement, they are evaluated and allocated numerical scores.

   In some cases even the answers on financial and economic standing will be allocated scores, but this is questionable when the test is one of adequacy.

Out of these rather turbid waters emerges a short-list which the purchaser hopes is comprised of the names of the six[73] (or so) best bidders. But who

71. If you are not confident about the quality of your policies look on the internet, there is plenty of advice to be found and even some model documents.

72. A nameless purchaser once engaged a nameless international accountancy practice to assist with the financial aspects of short-listing for a procurement of health services. A bidder submitted a duly signed letter of financial support from a lender who operated according to Sharia principles. The international accountancy practice recommended exclusion of the bidder because to them it didn't look like a bank, yet they recommended acceptance of others who had submitted copies of unendorsed e-mails stating simply that they held an account at a 'real' bank. When it was discovered this injustice was corrected and the bidder was brought back in to the procurement.

73. Six appears to be the magic number, and the Regulations (16(9b)) say that it can't be fewer than

knows what 'best' is at this stage? And the law of unintended consequences often strikes down the competent and selects the incompetent. Regardless of whether or not purchasers put the names in a hat, chance has its part to play.

- ***In a PQQ many questions are pass/fail or otherwise non-scoring (such as requests for names and addresses) so suppliers can lose a sense of proportion when allocating weights to the relatively few scoring questions. Look out for these imbalances and use them to your advantage. You may wish to expound at length on your technical ability, but this may not be worth as many points as your environmental policy.***
- ***Check whether minimum levels for financial standing or ability are specified in the notice and, if so, whether you can meet them;***
- ***if not, ask what the minimum levels are, but don't necessarily expect a coherent answer.***
- ***If you are excluded at the PQQ stage ask whether it was because you failed to meet the minimum levels. If they weren't specified and you allegedly failed to meet them, then you have possible grounds for challenge[74].***
- ***Most important of all, remember that there is a substantial element of chance about the PQQ evaluation process, so if you fail to reach a short-list don't take it too much to heart.***

How is the winning tender chosen?

Apart from listing the factors that may be taken into account the Regulations provide no guidance as to the process of assessing which is the most economically advantageous tender. It is up to each purchaser to design its own methodology and set its own priorities.

One possible approach might be adequacy, i.e. to set a level of quality that satisfies the purchaser's requirements, then, of the tenders that clear that bar, select the cheapest. Many purchasers go some way along this track, i.e. they set a level below which the standard of the offering set out in a tender

five. A short-list of six allows for one drop out, one no-hoper (there is usually at least one who creeps onto a short-list) and one in reserve so that, barring disasters, there will still be sufficient tenders to provide realistic competition.

74. But it would be something of a punt because the argument might hinge, for example, on whether a statement such as *the purchaser will use the information derived from questions about financial standing and technical capability* is such a specification.

is deemed inadequate[75], but they will not accept that adequate and cheapest is good enough for them.

In the same way as purchasers want the six or so 'best' suppliers on their short-list they also want the 'best' supplier to win the bid and feel that there is merit in paying more for more than adequate. But surely this is more than they previously (in the specification, perhaps) defined as what was needed, not to mention being a questionable way to spend taxpayer's money[76].

So if the purchaser is not going to select the lowest priced tender that clears the bar it is left with a problem. Which is more *economically advantageous*[77]: a low-priced tender with a low (but adequate) quality score or a high-priced tender with a high quality score?

The usual solution is to devise an algorithm that mashes a numerical score for price with the quality score to arrive at an overall score. Many weird and wonderful methods are invented and more than a few purchasers have run into trouble by failing to recognise the consequences of their arithmetic.

If there is no price ceiling and the algorithm gives insufficient weight to a competitive price then a 'high quality' tender with a high or even unaffordable price will score the most points. And as points mean prizes this can come as an uncomfortable shock to the purchaser.

One reasonably safe method of arriving at an overall score for each tender is as follows:

1. Start from the position where there is a price ceiling[78].
2. Define a split of the final score between price and quality, say 30:70 (the regulations are silent on this relationship and it is up to the purchaser to decide, but this ratio is fairly common[79]. Whether or not

75. For example the purchaser might say that, no matter what the overall score, if a bidder falls below, say. 50% on the clinical section of the tender then the bid is rejected.

76. 'Best' is a slippery concept and it is highly questionable whether this is what a PQQ or an ITT measures anyway. The author has advanced the adequacy approach on several occasions, but purchasers just don't like it (he has never dared to suggest a lottery at the PQQ stage). In this context it is worth considering the debate about standards in schools, where a rating of satisfactory seems to translate as damning criticism.

77. But is that the same as better value for money?

78. This should be made known in advance – see the section *Do purchasers have to tell you their budgetary limit or price ceiling?*

79. Those of an arithmetical bent will realise that there is no reason that scores should be expressed as percentages or add up to a hundred, but although (perhaps because) percentage sums seem to frighten some people, they carry more weight. And it has to be admitted that the result is often clearer if the final score is expressed as a percentage. For example expressing the winning margin as 5% has more meaning than saying the winner scored 265 points with the runner up scoring 230 points and leaving the total achievable score somewhat vague.

there is rational justification for it is another matter).

3. Place bid prices on a scale and award points in an inverse relationship to the position on the scale, i.e. the higher the price, the fewer the points. Thus the lowest price has the potential to score 30 points[80].
4. Convert the quality score to a value out of 70.
5. Add the quality score to the price score to give the overall score.
6. The tender with the highest overall score wins.

- ***Ensure that you understand fully the evaluation methodology before you prepare your submission. If there isn't enough information in the PQQ or ITT, then ask. You may receive enlightenment, but if you don't then think carefully about how you should proceed.***
- ***Test the arithmetic of the evaluation methodology – does it make sense? Not all purchasers are as numerate as you are.***
- ***If you don't reach the shortlist or having done so don't win, check that the published evaluation methodology was used in making the decision.***

Evaluating more complex bid prices

Not all ITTs ask for the bid price as a single number. Here we consider some of the issues that arise from more complex pricing schemes.

<u>Volume-related pricing</u>

Where the payment made by the purchaser is related to volume, the bidder needs to know what this volume is likely to be a) so that the bidder can estimate its own costs to arrive at a sensible bid price; and b) to understand how the bid price will be represented in the selection process.

Where there is only one unit of price[81] the bidder needs to know the number of units that will[82] be (or are likely to be) consumed and, if it is

80. Whether or not the lowest price scores 30 points depends on how the rules are defined – if the lower end of the scale is defined as the lowest price, then it will.

81. e.g. in dental contracts that are priced on the basis of a Unit of Dental Activity (UDA) and the various elements of the service (filling, extraction, etc) are each defined as being worth a specific number of UDAs.

82. Again taking the example of a dental contract the number of UDAs to be consumed is fixed within tight limits, so the bidder has a very clear idea of its costs, and so in this case it is quite reasonable for the purchaser to use the price per UDA in the evaluation process.

different, the number of units that will be used in calculating the price of the contract.

- ***The purchaser may have ulterior motives in setting the predicted usage of a service. Try to understand the purchaser's thinking about the projected volumes so that you can make a sensible estimation of your risks.***

Where an ITT asks for separate prices for different elements of the service the calculation of a single bid price becomes more complex. It is to be hoped that the purchaser has defined a pricing model where the quantities of each element of service are shown. Bidders should be allowed to see this model, but it is not beyond the bounds of possibility that the purchaser hasn't progressed that far at the ITT stage or wishes to withhold[83] its projected methodology.

- ***Especially where pricing is complex ensure that you understand how the purchaser will arrive at the number that goes into the bid price evaluation pot.***

Variable annual price

The total annual cost of services can vary over the life of the contract. It may be that the service is novel so usage will increase with acceptance or perhaps the price is front loaded to offset set-up costs.

This means that there is more than one way of arriving at the price used in the comparison and evaluation of bids. The simplest[84] is to sum the (projected) annual prices over the life of the contract; more sophisticated purchasers might add discounted cash flow into the calculations[85].

Especially in the case where the revenue from a contract is projected to increase with time there could be a significant (in terms of scoring) difference between the discounted and non-discounted price.

- ***If you have some flexibility as to how you price from year to year use it to make your bid price as competitive as possible.***
- ***Remember that the bid price that counts is the number that goes***

83. There is a (perhaps?) understandable reluctance on the part of some purchasers to reveal too much. Purchasers wish to be in charge and anyway telling the bidders too much will help them in their bid and might even enable them to bid a higher price than they would do if kept in ignorance. This may not sound logical, but …

84. It is to be hoped that a purchaser would base the calculation on the whole life cost or a proxy rather than, say, first year cost, but don't assume anything!

85. i.e. if the purchaser decides to apply the principle that money to be spent next year is worth less than money to be spent tomorrow.

into the evaluation pot, which may not be the single number or the sum of a set of numbers that you submit.

How do I price my bid?

The question on bid price is probably the most challenging in an ITT, especially if you don't have the experience of providing the service and/ or the resources to conduct a thorough analysis of your costs and the likely market. However, before you begin to formulate your answer you need to ask how much (or even whether) the bid price matters.

This seems a strange question, but either accidently or otherwise, some purchasers construct evaluation schemes that one way or the other place little emphasis on bid price.

- ***Establish how price will come into the calculations. It might matter a lot less than you think.***
- ***Use a spreadsheet to make a model of the scoring system and test price sensitivity for yourself.***
- ***If you discover a loophole think carefully before asking for clarification. It may be in your interests to exploit that loophole without alerting either the purchaser or your competitors.***
- ***But if you find that there is no real bar to a high bid price, don't overexploit it. For the purchaser there comes a point where the embarrassment of restarting the procurement is outweighed by the embarrassment of an unaffordable contract.***

In the majority of cases, however, the bid price carries a reasonable weight in the evaluation so you need to relate bid price to your costs. It is impossible to provide all-purpose guidance on how to price the bid, but there are a few points to bear in mind.

- ***The most important consideration when deciding on price is that you make a profit. The amount of profit required is up to you, but, if you don't think you can come up with a competitive price or meet any price constraints, don't bid. Better to walk away than risk taking on a loss-making contract***[86]***.***
- ***Don't assume that if the purchaser sets a price ceiling this is necessarily an achievable target. Purchasers can sometimes be quite naïve about costs.***

86. This is a statement of the obvious, but experience shows that it is a principle not always understood by bidders.

- ***If there is a clearly-expressed price ceiling, don't exceed it.***
- ***Try to score as many points on price as you can whilst still making a reasonable profit.***
- ***Even if it is not stated explicitly determine whether you can charge at different rates through the life of the contract so as to offset set-up costs and cash flow delays in the initial stages.***

Some ITTs contain financial schedules, usually in the form of spreadsheets which can be complex. They vary in the way they work but some go so far as to require you to plug in your staffing estimates, wage rates, rent and other costs plus profit margin and thereby work out your bid price for you.

- ***Treat with great caution complex spreadsheets that ask you for your costs and make sure that you understand what information they are seeking and for what reason.***
- ***Follow through any entries that you make to see what results they generate and ask whether these results make sense in your situation and are reflected in your bid price.***

One of the trickiest problems for a bidder is conversion of the purchaser's service level requirements[87] into staffing numbers. The wage bill is the major cost of most services, so getting this right is vital to the viability of your bid. Unfortunately, purchasers are not always as clear as they might be about their service levels, partly because they don't really understand the service, partly because they can't find a reasonable way of defining measures of performance.

The problem of balancing staff numbers against service demands is not just tricky, it is the Achilles heel of outsourcing public services by competitive tender. The purchaser doesn't specify the staff numbers to be provided, because a) it would be nonsense at the same time to lay down levels of service; and b) the whole point of outsourcing is to find the contractor who can operate the service more efficiently than the purchaser, so what does the purchaser know about staff numbers anyway?

87. e.g. for an out of hours GP service, where the time to respond target will be at best a guess informed by experience. But even requirements that should be expressible with clarity can be fudged. The centrally-defined specification for the Equitable Access to Primary Medical Care project (the procurement which set up the 'Darzi centres') contained a requirement for a GP to be 'available at all times'. Bidders asked does that mean on the premises, just down the road, or what? Several 'clarifications' were issued by the DH, none of which really settled the matter. As a result (and of several other instances of lack of clarity, it has to be admitted) some bidders tendered for twice as many GP hours as others.

- ***If you are making price calculations for a bid, you need to understand both your own financial position and the possible attitude of competitors. Regrettably there are bidders who will cut staffing to the bone for a low bid price and worry about the service levels later.***

Risk sharing – what is that about?

When PFI became the vogue there was much talk of risk transfer and risk sharing, but what the devisors of PFI conveniently underplayed was that there is a cost to bearing risk – an insurance premium if you like. Purchasers wishing to transfer risk found that bidders were canny and put a price on it.

Bidders would hold that the acceptance of some risks, such as change in law[88], were out of the question because the potential consequences were seen as unlimited and unlimitable; others, such as uncertainty about the number of transactions over the life of a contract, might be acceptable, but at a price.

By specifically pricing each risk bidders could in effect put pressure on sections of the specification. Faced with large numbers preceded by pound signs the purchaser usually backed down and took back responsibility for most of the risks. After all, the worst might not happen, but the invoices will always arrive[89].

- ***Does the contract require you to bear an element of risk?***
- ***If so, do you fully understand the possible implications of that risk?***
- ***The purchaser may not be as familiar[90] with the delivery of the service as you are – are you confident that the purchaser really understands what is involved in risk transfer?***
- ***Reducing risk reduces uncertainty and therefore your costs. How much can you transfer back to the purchaser?***
- ***Be aware that you may be bidding against someone who is gambling***

88. i.e. that at some time a law might change (or a new law might be introduced) and radically affect or even pull out the rug from under the contract. For example, Health and Safety Regulations might change to require that an operation previously conducted by one person has in future to be supervised by a safety officer, thus doubling staff costs.
89. Of course we cannot know the details of every outsourcing disaster over the years, but there do seem to be two major threads: failure of the contract mechanisms to detect and/or penalise underperformance and avoidance of risk by the contractor.
90. Especially if the procurement is being run by a procurement specialist who does not have practical knowledge of the operation of the service.

on being able to avoid the consequences of risk transfer and so does not price for it.

Performance indicators

It is clearly a Good Thing that a purchaser should measure whether a service is being delivered to a required standard and make payments for the service contingent on that standard being achieved. There are, however, three main problems (and many minor ones) for purchasers who attempt to define performance indicators[91] (PIs) and payment regimes:

- only that which is measurable can be measured, e.g. how do you measure skills like caring?
- if the purchaser is to define ways of measuring performance it needs to understand and be able to define every aspect of the service. Unfortunately there is a big difference between recognising a properly performing service when you see it and describing it in the precise and unambiguous manner required in a contractual performance regime[92] (let alone having the capacity to define every last detail); and
- the law of unintended consequences is always lurking round the corner with a banana skin at the ready to throw under the feet of anyone having the temerity to design a performance regime[93].

There are myriad examples of where PIs have gone wrong. Here are just a few.

<u>Carelessly defined performance indicator</u>

A major hospital let an IT support contract to a reputable supplier and PIs were included in the contract. Support was provided to users through a service desk and a PI measured the time that was taken to resolve calls made to the service desk. Users were highly critical of the standard of the support service,

91. A term often used is Key Performance Indicators (KPIs) but what is the point in a performance indicator that is not key?

92. Admittedly chunks of a definition can be dispensed with by methods such as depending on a contractor being a member of a profession and so governed by the standards of the regulating body or by a formula such as requiring that contractors *conduct their work with the degree of skill that could be reasonably expected of someone in their profession,* but to a certain extent these are cop-outs because they still leave many aspects of service delivery uncovered.

93. You only have to consider the controversy that targets in health care have aroused to see that not all performance targets encourage the desired result.

particularly the time taken to fix faults, but the contractor claimed that it had *consistently met or exceeded the required levels of service.*

The users' opinion of the service was entirely justified, but at the same time the contractor was telling the truth. Why? Because calls about real faults were diluted almost to the point of invisibility by a huge number of relatively trivial and easily resolved calls that weren't really about faults at all. In calculating performance all types of call stood on the same footing, so fixing a broken computer or application carried the same weight as resetting a lost password.

A quick turnaround on sorting out forgotten passwords and the like guaranteed that 95% of calls were easily resolved within the target time of twenty minutes. Add to this the absence of a maximum resolution time for fault calls (which meant intractable problems could be rolled over month by month without the supplier being penalised) and it was hardly surprising that users were less than satisfied whilst the contractor went unpunished.

Following the rules literally

Letters kept appearing in the press criticising the performance of a local authority's telephone service. Callers complained that they were kept hanging on for half-an-hour or more. The authority commissioned a survey of its switchboard. The consultant listened in to calls, timed responses and found the service to be impeccable – prompt, friendly and informative. As he looked around he saw a PC in the corner that displayed a moving graph.

He enquired. It turned out that the revenues and benefits (council tax, housing benefit, etc.) department had been contracted out and had its own telephone numbers that bypassed the switchboard. The PC showed how long callers were waiting on those numbers. The letters of complaint were not exaggerated – at that very moment one caller had been hanging on for forty minutes.

How could this be? A PI in the contract required that 95% of calls must be answered in less than 30 seconds. And every call was answered in less than 30 seconds – by an auto answer system. Waiting to speak to a human being took little longer.

Of course, it was the time that the machine took to answer that was quoted in the performance reports and under the terms of the contract there was little that the council could do, although all concerned knew what was really required.

Perverse incentives

A couple of years ago the Department of Health (DH) developed the PDS Plus contract for dental services. Short of having an expert standing at the dentist's elbow as he works, it is difficult to devise PIs that measure proficiency of execution, so the relevant PIs in the contract were measures of effect.

One PI measured whether patients returned for remedial treatment for a problem that had already been treated. The DH saw it as an indicator of poor practice if, for example, a tooth was filled and within a few months the filling failed so that the patient had to return for an extraction. This might be reasonable in some circumstances, but dentists asked why they should attempt to save a tooth by filling if they risked losing money if the filling subsequently failed.

The effect of this PI was that if there was any doubt about the viability of the tooth the 'safe' procedure was to extract immediately. The DH's intention was well meaning, but in practicing conservative dentistry practitioners risked being penalised.

The difficulty faced by purchasers in defining and measuring PIs probably works in favour of the contractor, but nevertheless you need to be wary when you are putting a bid together. Study the PIs carefully and think about how they would impact delivery of the service and the price that you will need to charge.

- ***How much does performance against PIs contribute to the total revenue from the contract, i.e. does it matter if you miss them occasionally?***
- ***Are PIs measuring anything of significance, i.e. would you be doing it to that standard anyway?***
- ***Look carefully at what the PIs are promoting. There may be an easy way to meet them, but are they in line with your professional standards? Could the PIs even distort the level of service? Could you find yourself consistently meeting or exceeding the required level of service, but being thrown out when the contract expires because of users' perceptions?***

- *Beware of PIs that are outside your control, especially those based on customer satisfaction surveys. A user/customer may be dissatisfied with the purchaser for reasons that are nothing to do with the part of the service that you run, and a questionnaire is the customer's opportunity to hit back.*
- *The law does not allow the purchaser to impose punitive charges on the contractor – any repayment by the contractor must reflect the loss to the purchaser resulting from the failure of the service. If the PIs appear to be punitive you may wish to discount them on the grounds that if the purchaser later attempts to rely on them they will prove unenforceable.*
- *Are the PIs backed up with a mechanism for terminating the contract for repeated 'failure'? If so, then take careful notice.*
- *Given the issues surrounding PIs the threat of termination is often the only viable tool for enforcing compliance but it is a huge step for the purchaser to take.*
- *Be aware that you may be bidding against a competitor that has based its price on just scraping through against PIs or has even seen an exploitable weakness in the mechanisms.*
- *Beware of regimes where the PIs get stricter from year to year. Can you really step up your performance that much? If you consider it too difficult, how about the other bidders? Will they just ignore the stricter requirements in the expectation that they can be renegotiated or won't be enforced?*
- *Ignore any implications in an ITT or contract that the purchaser reserves the right to change or add to PIs during the life of the contract. If a PI or a value attached to a PI is not explicitly defined in the contract that you sign it cannot be added or changed later without your consent, which you are perfectly entitled to withhold.*
- *Most PI regimes have a bedding-in period where there is a moratorium on PIs[94]. Plan to use this to your advantage, but don't plan to give a bad impression from the start.*

When considering the above it is worth bearing in mind the real world in which purchasers operate:

94. For example you are paid as if you have achieved them whether or not you have done so.

- once the contract is in place management of it is often seen by the purchaser as an optional and expensive extra. Until something goes wrong, that is;
- the contract manager's day-to-day interaction with the service provider's staff engenders a degree of sympathy with their problems. In fact they may have been colleagues before the service was outsourced; and
- a PI regime might look good on paper, but if a contractor isn't performing satisfactorily the threat of premature termination of the contract is the only real tool in a purchaser's armoury, especially if the contractor is happy to live with the associated loss of revenue.

  Premature termination is a huge step for the purchaser. The contractor might put up a legal fight in which the PI regime will be tested to breaking point, but worse still premature termination is seen as an admission of multiple failures by the purchaser: the design of the contract was less than perfect; the selection of the contractor was flawed; the contract was not properly supervised. In consequence purchasers often prefer to blunder on rather than face the legal costs and bad publicity that go with the nuclear option of termination.

The problem with questions

Elsewhere in this book we refer to the limitations of the question and answer dialogue as a method of measuring and predicting the relative merits of proposals for the supply of a service. But the limitations of the method are not the only problem for the purchaser. Even where the dialogue has direct relevance it is far from easy to assemble a respectable set of questions.

The project manager, it is to be hoped, is skilled in writing procurement documents, but he or she will not necessarily have a detailed knowledge of the whole of the service, if indeed of any part of it. For the most part the project manager is dependent on others to set the questions[95] that test a bidder's capabilities (in the PQQ) and the quality of the proposed service (in the ITT).

95. It is possible that the project manager will also be assembling a service specification that describes the purchaser's requirement for bidders and that will eventually form part of the contract. Presumably this is a skill that the project manager also possesses, but equivalent problems arise with this task also. There is a wide gap between a purchaser knowing what it wants and being able to describe it unambiguously and in full so that, in the extreme, a court could use the description to test whether the contractor had delivered or not.

There will be many people willing to suggest a subject for enquiry, but there is a big gap between making a suggestion and framing a question. In an ITT, for example, to be of any use, a question must test the likelihood of a particular characteristic of the service being delivered to a required standard by eliciting a relevant and measurable[96] answer. And along with the question must come appropriate scoring guidance.

One question is not enough. Several sets are required, each of which deals with a major aspect of the characteristics of the bidder or the service. No set of questions in a PQQ or an ITT will be perfect, but at their worst they can be the product of a project manager who is grateful for any questions however poorly expressed so long as he or she can tweak them into some sort of respectability.

- ***Don't be surprised if the questions do not cover all aspects of the purchaser's requirement or even appear to be peripheral to its main aspects. There is nothing you can do to change the questions so look to score points on what you have in front of you, not what you would like to see there.***
- ***In theory, and if the purchaser is playing strictly by the rules, you should not be able to score points for mentioning something in an answer that you haven't been asked about. Nevertheless, if you feel that the questions do not allow you to address some of your strong points it might be worth mentioning these anyway. Choose the question of nearest relevance[97], but be brief.***

Bidder presentations – what are they for?

The short answer is that most purchasers aren't really sure. The Regulations are silent on the subject of bidder presentations so it is hardly surprising that they are a cause of confusion and that the easiest way to avoid the problem is not to hold them at all.

96. Measurability demands that the response is capable of being graded AND that those grades have some relationship to the requirement.

97. And if the PQQ/ITT is divided into sections, think about the people who will be marking each section and aim to impress the person who will understand and appreciate what you wish to say. It has to be admitted that this is not an easy tactic on which to give advice, because it essentially relies on the purchaser disregarding best practice, i.e. awarding points that are not justified by the scoring guidance and/or being favourably influenced by your words so that a generally sympathetic approach to marking is adopted, but sentiments such as *I quite like this bidder because it mentioned x even though we didn't ask about x* are not unknown amongst evaluators.

The problem with most bidder presentations is that purchasers tend to delay deciding their place in the process until the last minute (sometimes when someone says *shouldn't we take a look at these people if we are going to work with one of them?*). Clear thinking and careful planning are not in abundance where presentations are concerned and the result can be confused and potentially inequitable.

Presentations only make sense at the award (ITT) stage[98] where there are three basic ways of fitting them into the process. The first and most sensible is to define the presentation as independent of the other aspects of the evaluation, accounting for, say, 10% of the quality score and having no impact on the scoring of the written response. This can be done, for example, by asking bidders to deliver their presentation on a particular aspect of the service that is perhaps better covered in this way than in a written response.

A slightly less sensible way is to use the presentation as a vehicle for the purchaser to modify or moderate its evaluation of the written response, but there are multiple dangers in this approach, including:

- can all evaluators of the tender attend every presentation? This is a huge investment of time, but if there isn't a full complement at every presentation then how is the process equitable?
- is every bidder asked the same set of questions at the presentation?
- does the questioning concentrate on the perceived strengths or weaknesses of the particular bidder? and
- what if the presentation is significantly at odds with the written response? Which takes precedence[99]? What if the final presentation raises an issue common to all tenders – do you call each of them back in again for questioning?

And, regrettably, there is the third way. This is where senior people are invited to attend the presentation because selecting a service supplier is an important decision for the organisation[100]. As senior people they have not

98. It is not forbidden to hold presentations at the selection (PQQ) stage, but it is unlikely that they would provide much more enlightenment than a good PQQ would. The problem for the purchaser, of course, would be that every prospective bidder would have to be given a chance and no one wants to listen to sixty presentations!

99. Admittedly, this issue can also arise with the first method if the topic of the presentation overlaps, either deliberately or accidentally, matters covered in the written questions.

100. And they might go on to say it's really about the people with whom you may be working and the only way to make this judgement is face-to-face, etc, etc.

had the time to do the hard slog of evaluation, so reconciling the views that they derive from a presentation with the results of a question-by-question evaluation of the tender can be problematic.

The fabled warm feeling can and does clash with the results of the methodical scoring process[101].

- ***If presentations are used make sure that you know how they will influence the scoring and plan your strategy accordingly. The purchaser should define in advance a protocol for running and scoring the presentations, but don't count on it.***
- ***Decide how much effort you are prepared to invest. Is it really worth taking much trouble if the presentation is worth only, say, 5% of the total score? On the other hand all might (rightly or wrongly) depend on the presentation, so should you concentrate considerable efforts here?***
- ***Anything that smacks of negotiation is banned in the Restricted procedure, so presentations are not an opportunity for sounding out the purchaser or offering a few extras to sweeten the contract. Beware of any situation that hints at negotiation; this would make the process subject to challenge.***
- ***Generally[102], a sensible purchaser will place more weight on a workmanlike presentation given by the people who will actually be delivering the service than on a slick delivery by, say, the area sales manager.***
- ***But above all, remember that the presentation is the most subjective aspect of the procurement process and few purchasers are able to handle it dispassionately. The above advice is (more or less) appropriate for a rational purchaser, but not all purchasers act rationally all of the time.***

What really counts?

Having already addressed the various matters above this might seem a strange question, but consider things from the purchaser's point of view.

101. It is not unknown for a chief executive having been charmed by a presentation to ask for the decision to be reviewed so that his or her views can have weight. But what does the ability to do a good presentation have to do with delivering the service?

102. As for all generalisations this is not always true.

The project has begun with the best and purest of intentions: outsourcing will bring in private sector skills that will reduce costs and improve the service; only the best will do but at the lowest cost; we don't want to do it the same old way as before so innovation must be rewarded; staff numbers aren't our concern – only the level of service; risk – that's for the successful bidder to worry about now; and so it goes.

These and similar sentiments underpin the definition of the requirement as set out in the ITT or an allied document, representing as they do the purchaser's opinions, desires and ambitions. But will they, or rather their observance, be the factors that distinguish the winner from the losers?

Well, up to a point. By adopting the output-based approach[103], which is the proper basis for the definition of a service requirement and the evaluation of proposals, it should be possible to keep these sentiments to the fore, but nevertheless they can often go missing. It's easy to express them, not so easy to translate them into a common thread that runs through the ITT questions and their associated evaluation criteria.

An example of this failure to reflect a high flown requirement occurred in the Dental Access Project[104]. In the early documents that described the proposed project, and indeed in the narrative parts of the centrally-devised procurement documentation, much was made of the desirability of an 'innovative' approach to delivery of NHS dental services.

The questions in the centrally-devised ITT, however, barely addressed innovation and the evaluation guidance not at all. Consequently few bidders proposed significant innovation nor, in the rare event of it being proposed, was it rewarded to any significant extent, if at all, by purchasers. The contracts were awarded to bidders who demonstrated value for money in conventional terms.

- ***Study all of the documentation associated with the procurement. If sentiments are expressed that do not appear to be reflected in the questions or the evaluation guidance, then consider seeking clarification.***

---

103. This might crudely be characterised as: *it is not for us to say how you do it; our concern is that the service that you propose will meet our needs.*

104. A DH initiative to increase the availability of NHS dentistry by a nationwide programme of competitive tendering. Outline procurement documentation which included PQQ and ITT questions was produced by the DH and made available for commissioners to 'tailor' to their own needs. Evaluation criteria were also produced centrally (but a little late to be useful to many of the local procurement projects).

- ***If the purchaser has stated, in one way or another, high level sentiments or requirements, then reflect them where possible in your answers, but your primary task must be to answer each question as posed and meet the demands, if known, of the evaluation guidance.***

New entrants

In days long ago when computers with processing capability less than a mobile phone would fill a large room and needed a small power station to supply their electricity[105] there was a saying that no one would be fired for buying IBM[106]. This was not hyperbole. IBM's computer systems[107] tended to be clunkier and more expensive than their rivals, but they dominated the market in a way that seems inconceivable now[108].

Procurement, especially public procurement, has changed a lot since those days, but the *buy from the big boys* attitude still haunts the minds of purchasers. The evaluation scheme might be well designed and rational, but that doesn't necessarily mean that someone somewhere in the organisation will not ask whether the decision is 'safe'. And by 'safe' they often mean a large and established supplier.

There is much bluster from the EU about making the procurement environment more favourable for Small and Medium Enterprises (SMEs). Regrettably, there is little evidence that anything substantive has been done and even less that this righteous cause has been taken up by purchasers of public services.

Admittedly the Regulations require that criteria for the assessment of the standing and experience of suppliers are *relevant and proportionate to the subject matter of the contract*[109] but this is a difficult judgement

105. Not all of what was just said in this sentence is strictly true.

106. An historical note: back in the 90s there was a then notorious scandal at Wessex Regional Health Authority when IBM computers lay about in boxes unused and millions of pounds were wasted. Even so no one responsible was actually sacked; they either stayed in post or in the best traditions of the NHS they were given substantial redundancy payments and moved on to better things elsewhere in the organisation.

107. In those days system effectively meant hardware and software supplied as a package.

108. So much so that their competitors were known as the seven dwarves.

109. Regulation 16(12) of the Public Contracts Regulations 2006.

for purchasers. And if purchasers find that more bidders have cleared the bar than there are places on the short-list, then they are entitled to use the distance by which the bar has been cleared as a criterion for selecting the short-list.

Whether or not you are capable of doing the job there is little point in wasting your time on bidding if the purchaser has different ideas:

- ***Inspect the selection questions carefully.***
- ***Find out what criteria will be used to assess experience. If there is a possibility they will rule you out, but nevertheless they appear relevant and proportionate, then you need to think about whether you continue.***
- ***If the selection criteria seem to rule you out, but you consider them neither relevant nor proportionate, then raise this with the purchaser. If the purchaser sticks with the criteria then again you must make a decision about continuing. In this case you might have grounds for a legal challenge, but is it worth the effort and expense?***

Experience is considered at the selection (PQQ) stage, so by definition if you make the short-list then you have adequate experience. Unfortunately, just to be sure some purchasers like to ask again at the ITT stage. Although contrary to the Regulations this is difficult to counter if the purchaser has a mind to do it. If you feel that you are light on experience a second round of questioning will not be in your interests.

- ***You might be able to head off the reassessment of experience by asking a direct question such as 'can you assure me that experience will not be an evaluation criterion at the award stage too?***

It seems to be an inevitable but perverse consequence of the equitable principle rule that established and experienced suppliers have the edge over new entrants[110]. It is the author's experience, however, that this perceived advantage breeds a degree of complacency that results in established (and especially large corporate) suppliers shooting themselves in their feet.

Typical examples of this complacency are: expecting the purchaser to accept an assertion that the bidder is the best thing since sliced bread without

110. Thus reducing the degree of competition, but it is beyond the scope of this book to any make definitive statements as to the influence of public procurement processes on markets for services save to mention the tendency of mature markets to approach a state of oligopoly.

any evidence to prove the claim; recycling the same bland, boilerplate answer from procurement to procurement, whether or not it is appropriate to the question; and lack of diligence in preparing responses – perhaps because they were based on that much-repeated boilerplate text – with answers being peppered with spelling errors and sentences that end half-way through.

- ***Do not be intimidated by being up against competition from big, well-established suppliers.***
- ***Having taken all of the above into account, if as a new entrant you go ahead with a bid then you give yourself the best chance by paying scrupulous care to every aspect of your submission.***
- ***Don't lose hope. Remain confident.***

Who is the bidder?

It is not unusual for a special entity in the form of a company, partnership, consortium or other grouping to be put together specifically for the purposes of bidding. Frequently, probably more often than not, these entities will not be incorporated at the PQQ stage[111] so the bidding vehicle is at best an empty vessel with no economic or technical history and usually it is a ghost ship. So who in such circumstances is the bidder and what is its experience?

One problem is the nature of legal personality[112]. Consider where an individual (a human being) normally does business through a limited company, but is a member of the consortium as an individual. Is it reasonable that he or she puts forward the accounts of the limited company as evidence of financial standing or cites the company's experience as the experience of the consortium?

Continued membership of a consortium also poses a problem. Again consider where A, B, C and D bid as a consortium that will be formally incorporated if they win the contract. The experience and/or financial standing of A, the strongest member, has been a major factor in the purchaser's considerations at the selection stage, but late in the procurement process A leaves the consortium.

A's desertion may not be drawn to the purchaser's attention and in this state

111. And often not at all unless the bid is successful.

112 i.e. if a human being (*natural person* in lawyer-speak) sets up a limited company (or other form of incorporation) even though the human being may own 100% of the shares in the company, the human being and the company are separate entities in the eyes of the law so can be sued, bankrupted, enter into contracts, etc separately and independently from one another.

of ignorance the purchaser goes on to award the contract to the consortium. It is only when pens are poised over the dotted lines that A's absence becomes apparent. What does the purchaser do? The easiest course is to ignore A's absence and carry on for the alternative might be to begin the procurement again from scratch[113].

The law offers no assistance on these matters so purchasers have to do the best they can. It is difficult to provide firm advice in such a cloudy area either on using a specially formed bidding vehicle or what to do if you are bidding against one, but the following should be considered.

- ***If you have formed or propose to form a bidding vehicle then, unless the purchaser has made definitive statements to the contrary, it is probably satisfactory to rely on the technical, legal and financial records of members at the PPQ stage.***
- ***These are difficult issues for purchasers, so if you are using a specially formed bidding vehicle and lack of clarity seems to allow you licence in what you submit about financial standing or experience, think carefully whether you need to ask for clarification. Why turn over stones unnecessarily?***
- ***Check the applicability of the PQQ questions. Can you put forward the experience of your 'best' member as the experience of the bidding entity? Are you really required to mention that unfortunate misunderstanding that another member had with the taxman a few years ago?***
- ***On the other hand, if you are bidding as an existing entity with its own record, but believe that other bidders are specially formed consortia then ask questions to ensure that you know, and more importantly the purchaser knows, what rules will be applied. This <u>is</u> the situation in which to turn over those stones.***
- ***If you have bid against and lost to a multi-member entity, then it's worth asking whether the membership has remained unchanged through the course of the procurement. If there has been desertion you may possibly have grounds for challenge, but you might find***

113. This is desertion at its most extreme. A's experience and standing doesn't have to be the major factor in the selection process for its desertion to weaken the consortium to the point where the consortium's suitability should be questioned.

yourself breaking new legal ground if you do so.

TUPE

In full TUPE[114] is the Transfer of Undertakings (Protection of Employment) Regulations 2006. Legal textbooks are devoted to it, and as is repeated several times herein, this is not a legal textbook. Here we can touch only on the basics and the immediate implications of TUPE for the bidder.

The underlying principle of TUPE is that if there is a transfer of undertaking from one employer to another then the staff engaged in the provision of that undertaking have certain rights to continued employment with whoever takes over the undertaking[115]. This means that if you win a contract and there are already staff in place (whether employed by the purchaser or an incumbent contractor) and they are providing more or less the same service as you will be providing, then those staff have the right to work for you.

From the point of view of a bidder, TUPE is both a Good Thing and a Bad Thing. Good, because there is already a competent (you hope) and experienced group of staff who will enable you to make a seamless transition.

Bad, because staff are not obliged to make any commitment until day one of the new contract, thus making the planning of recruitment rather tricky. Bad also, because it might be that the incumbent supplier lost the contract because its staff were providing a poor service, or for a first-time outsourcing of the service, because outsourcing was seen as an easy answer to poor performance.

- ***TUPE rights belong to the employees. Statements by the purchaser such as 'there will be no TUPE transfers[116]' have no value – the purchaser cannot override the law. If a purchaser makes such a claim ask to be indemnified against the claim turning out to be***

114. Usually pronounced 2P or thereabouts.

115. The law is, of course, much more complex than this. The employee does not acquire the right to be employed for ever. Questions arise such what is the undertaking exactly? How much of it is being transferred? What proportion of their time do the staff devote to those aspects of the undertaking that is being transferred? Pensions are a particularly dangerous area, given the increasing superiority of public sector pensions over those offered by the private sector. Transferring employees are entitled to *broadly comparable* pension arrangements which can prove to be very expensive (and possibly divisive if others of your staff have different arrangements). All of which only goes to show how much we need lawyers.

116. A statement allegedly made, with table thumping emphasis, by the project director of an overambitious and under delivering NHS outsourcing project.

false.

- ***Wise purchasers will make preparations and provide full information on any staff entitled to transfer under TUPE. If you suspect that there may be staff who have rights of transfer under TUPE make sure that you are provided with this information and factor it in to your proposals and costs (as best you can).***
- ***If you are in doubt about any of the TUPE information provided by the purchaser ask to be indemnified against any unplanned costs that you might suffer should the information prove incorrect (it's probably best to be indemnified for unexpected TUPE costs in any circumstance).***

Bidding against an incumbent supplier

The end date of a service contract is approaching[117] so a project is launched to re-procure. What is the position of the incumbent supplier and, considering its wealth of inside knowledge, is it worth bidding against it?

There is no process that can truly level the playing field if an incumbent supplier is bidding to be re-awarded the contract. Just to give four of many reasons: the incumbent will have a clear picture of the risks inherent in the contract and will be better placed to factor them into its price; it will probably have already recovered many of its set-up costs giving it a cost advantage over its competitors; it will know the current staff and can be more confident that they will remain in place than if a new provider took over; and, regrettable but true, the incumbent will know the purchaser, how strong the contract management is and what a contractor can get away with[118].

The purchaser's view also tilts the playing field. Whether towards or against the incumbent depends on whether familiarity has bred contempt or it is the devil that the purchaser knows[119]. The purchaser will always have more information about the incumbent and its operations than are revealed in the incumbent's bid. What if the incumbent makes claims that

117. Often, because of inertia on the part of the purchaser, much too rapidly. As Douglas Adams said: 'I love deadlines. I like the whooshing sound they make as they fly by'.

118. The advantages of being the incumbent were starkly illustrated by Virgin's bid for the National Lottery contract in 1999. Even the saintly Richard Branson proved unable to oust Camelot.

119. And, viewed solely from the point of view of the taxpayer, what is wrong with going for the safe option, provided that the price is reasonable?

the purchaser knows from experience are exaggerated or even untrue? On the face of it this is a case for a specific clarification question, but this is dangerous territory with regard to equitable treatment.

And what if the incumbent understates its virtues – does the purchaser award a score for the answer or for what it knows from experience? Evaluation must be on the basis of the answer, of course, but evaluators are human and can't temporarily forget what they know. They want to do the best for their organisation so there is a strong temptation to use all information at their disposal from whatever source.

Even when incumbents are held in deep contempt it doesn't mean that the purchaser will cast them from the procurement process at the earliest opportunity. It is impossible to know how often it happens, but an unsatisfactory incumbent is sometimes strung along on the grounds that as soon as it learns it has no chance of renewal it will lose interest for the remaining life of the contract and the service will deteriorate further.

- ***If you are competing against an incumbent supplier ask what precautions the purchaser has taken to ensure equitable treatment, particularly with regard to the supply of documentation and other information to bidders.***
- ***Beware, the purchaser may put up the smokescreen of commercial confidentiality if you ask to see documents relating to an existing contract. Whether something is commercially confidential or not depends very much on the standpoint of the viewer[120] so you may need to consider taking legal advice.***
- ***Do what you can to monitor the procurement process and raise any potential issues of inequity as soon as they become apparent.***
- ***However, if you are short-listed alongside the incumbent supplier look on the bright side. It might mean there is be one viable competitor fewer!***

Bidding as an incumbent supplier

When a service is re-procured it is unlikely that the specification will be recycled without being changed in some way; even so the incumbent

120. And the context. If knowledge of information gives the incumbent an advantage over competitors then the smokescreen must be blown away.

supplier will be expected to bid and should expect to be shortlisted (at least). Nevertheless, bidding as an incumbent has its problems:

- competitors see an incumbent as being on the inside track, a suspicion which would of course be seen to be confirmed if the incumbent were to win;
- the incumbent's staff currently delivering the service will be unsettled by the uncertainty as to who their employer will be in a few months (and at some stage may even be interviewed by the competition to size them up for TUPE transfer[121]);
- the incumbent is sometimes required to pass information about the current service to the competition – cue an argument about protection of commercial secrets;
- the purchaser knows (or thinks it knows) the faults and weaknesses of the incumbent, whereas competitors reveal only their best sides;
- an incumbent is in something of a bind when putting together its bid team. The incumbent's service manager could be outshone by the competition's specialist bid managers, and in the view of the customer might even carry baggage; on the other hand the purchaser might expect a plain, straightforward approach; and
- the incumbent's working relationship with the purchaser will become formal and perhaps strained as the procurement proceeds.

However, an incumbent should not overlook the advantages of its position:

- lower set-up costs and lower TUPE risks can be reflected in a competitive bid price;
- the outgoing contract has been a live test of local conditions; and
- there is already a working relationship with the purchaser.

It is in the nature of human beings that the procurement process does not operate totally mechanistically, especially when there is a relationship already in existence. Whatever the Regulations might say it is unlikely that the incumbent's performance of the outgoing contract will not come into the evaluation in some way.

- ***Nevertheless, an incumbent should not assume that any gaps left in its proposals will be filled by the purchaser. Just like everyone***

121. The incumbent's staff have the right to TUPE transfer and to maintain their working conditions, but the competitors will wish to assess what they are getting and how likely the employees are to stay in post.

else an incumbent must be judged only on its responses to the PQQ and ITT (and possibly its presentation).

- ***The worst sin an incumbent can commit is to appear over-confident – this is the quickest way to alienate evaluators.***
- ***It is generally better to admit to any problems with the outgoing service and say how they will be avoided in future than to try to argue them away.***
- ***Think carefully about your bid team, especially if there are to be formal presentations. Are the members of your team currently providing the service an asset or an encumbrance (a question that can only be answered if you know and understand both your people and your customer)?***
- ***It would be a fool of a project manager who 'allowed' an unsatisfactory incumbent to win. Good impressions are made throughout the life of the service. An incumbent can't turn perceptions around by making an effort in the last few months – if anything that shines a brighter light on the earlier poor performance.***
- ***An incumbent must beware of perceptions over-riding actuality and being saddled with the blame for shortcomings that are outside its control and/or even outside the scope of the contract[122].***
- ***An incumbent's view of the standard of its service can be at odds with that of the users of the service, which in turn may differ from that of the purchaser[123]. The incumbent must establish and face up to whichever version the purchaser will hold to be the truth at the time of the procurement (which may even mean that bidding is a waste of time).***

This clash of views can throw up some interesting dilemmas. Consider for instance dental premises. A dentist may have been delivering services from his or her existing premises for several years without complaint or comment

122. Where the contract is for, say, a service where requests come through a call centre that is not under the control of the service provider. If the call centre service is poor, then the perception will be that the service is poor.

123. This happens. There are many possible reasons, including: reliance on the wrong performance indicators; users misunderstanding the service; wilful ignorance on the part of the incumbent; misreporting by interested parties; contract managers who have lost the plot.

from the purchaser (commissioner). The dentist then bids against other dentists to provide additional services[124].

One of the factors examined in the ITT is the standard of premises proposed for delivering the services. The dentist's answers to the question on premises are naturally based on the current premises. The competitors' answers, however, are: a) based on premises that may not have been secured at the time of the tender (and therefore should a competitor win it may not use the proposed premises); and b) presented as architectural drawings.

The dentist's problem is that his or her premises, although not having given cause for comment during the course of the contract, may be rated as only adequate by the purchaser (scoring, say three points). The competitors have no such problems, for (if they have any sense) they will have instructed their architects to produce elegant drawings that satisfy every possible requirement and so pictures beat brickwork by five points to three.

It is in situations like this where the incumbent supplier really needs to know its customer and the detailed requirements for the procurement.

- ***As an incumbent supplier do not assume that silence implies satisfaction. You should seek feedback from the customer, particularly the decision makers, and from users throughout the life of the contract.***
- ***Improve your services throughout the life of the contract and look for somewhere in your tender where you can underline your achievements.***
- ***Do not assume that a re-procurement is seeking more of the same. Find out how the requirements have changed and seek to explain what you will do to upgrade your services to meet the new requirements.***

If I lose a procurement can I charge for my wasted time?

No, but see the next section.

What can I do if a procurement is abandoned?

Wise purchasers cover themselves with early and explicit caveats that they

124. This is not the place to debate whether or not it is legitimate to engineer time limits into dental contracts, but for the purposes of this illustration it matters not whether this is additional work or a re-procurement of the current service.

reserve the right to cancel the procurement at any time for any reason and that they are not obliged to appoint a contractor at all if they don't want to.

This prompts the question of why, having gone to all of the trouble to set up a procurement project, would the purchaser then cancel it? There are a number of possible explanations, some reasonable, some less so, including:

- the purchaser realises that it has made a mess of the process[125] and it is open to challenge or might just end up with the 'wrong' result;
- budgets have been hacked away since the procurement began;
- organisational structures have changed;
- there has been a change of government policy or even a change of law; or
- bids have turned out to be unaffordable.

But what can you do, having wasted your time and effort? The caveats only stand if the purchaser has behaved reasonably, but if you consider the behaviour unreasonable there is not a lot that you can do unless you are prepared to enter the legal casino. Even if you win it is unlikely that you would recover more than your bidding costs.

- ***A declaration of no contest is just another outcome that you risk when you enter a procurement contest.***

What is a framework agreement?

A Google search for an answer to this question finds: *a quick & easy way of procuring supplies or services, which can also save on procurement costs!* (the exclamation mark is part of the quote). Certainly this is what frameworks ought to be, but for services (but not necessarily for supplies) it is far from clear whether in practice they are worthwhile for either suppliers or purchasers.

The Government Procurement Service[126] is the department that currently has central responsibility for framework agreements. It has inherited or set up numerous framework agreements for goods and services for use by most public sector bodies (although the existence of centralised framework agreements does not necessarily preclude public sector bodies from setting up their own frameworks).

125. Often right at the start with a flawed notice in the OJEU because the purchaser was in a hurry and thought it could save time with an early notice, but the West Coast Mainline debacle in 2012 demonstrated that it can come anywhere in the process.

126. http://gps.cabinetoffice.gov.uk

A convenient way to think of a framework is as semi-permanent short-list analogous to that following the PQQ stage of a Restricted procedure. Briefly, framework agreements work as follows:

- a public body initiates the procurement of a framework agreement by placing a notice in the OJEU;
- the notice must state the nature of the goods or services required and specify the bodies or class of bodies who will be able to use the framework once established;
- applicants submit responses to what is effectively a PQQ and those who get the questions right and/or score highly enough qualify as framework suppliers;
- a public body contemplating a procurement selects a framework agreement that covers its requirement and then:
    - if on the basis of the information in the framework agreement a particular supplier can be identified as the best for the requirement, award the contract directly to that supplier; or
    - if it is not possible to identify the supplier in that way run a *mini-competition* between the members of the framework[127];
- the terms of the resulting contract are substantially those set out in the original procurement of the framework. Depending on how effectively the framework has been set up this may be a few sheets of paper or a full-blown agreement; and
- the framework agreement itself should not last more than four years, but this does not prevent contracts established under a framework living beyond the four-year period.

Superficially, frameworks seem to be a jolly fine idea. They dispense with the red-tape of a full OJEU-originating procurement; they guarantee good prices; they present the purchaser with a ready-made list of pre-qualified and suitably experienced suppliers; and they put the chosen suppliers in a privileged position. But there is another way of looking at them, especially frameworks for services:

- the speed advantage isn't always as great as it might seem – purchasers must still draw up a full specification of the requirement and run the second part (effectively ITT) of the procurement;

127. Advice on the choice of suppliers for mini-competition varies; some authorities say approach all bidders, others say select, say, three and ask them to submit proposals.

- the process of selection of a supplier must still observe the principles and applicable rules of the Regulations[128];
- markets, technology and prices change quickly, but the membership and conditions of a framework are fixed for its (usually) four-year life; and
- there is a tendency for the large general-purpose organisations who can afford to spend time on qualifying to shoulder out the smaller specialist organisations[129].

Central government bodies are 'mandated' to use frameworks[130] for low to medium value procurements (but in what manner or how rigidly that mandation is enforced is not known). Other public bodies are not obliged to use frameworks, and many suppliers would hold that they are not the guaranteed stream of work that they might seem.

- ***Think carefully about bidding to take part in a framework agreement. Many organisations have regretted the time and money wasted on qualifying when they find that the phone rings no more frequently than it did before.***

The shift in the balance of power

At the beginning of a procurement process the purchaser is very much in the driving seat and, within reason, what it says goes. The purchaser sets the timescales, sets times and dates for bidder seminars and bidder presentations and makes all manner of other rulings with which bidders must comply or be thrown out[131]. A bidder crosses the purchaser at its peril.

It is not always recognised, however, that as the procurement proceeds the balance of power shifts. Although as a bidder you might not wish to take

128. Nevertheless having had no part in the pre-selection there is a strong temptation for purchasers to defy the Regulations and re-examine the bidders' experience for themselves.

129. Where there are multiple frameworks for different flavours of a high-level requirement (e.g. consultancy is subdivided into such as IT, management, strategic, procurement, etc) it is interesting to see the names of the same large multi-discipline organisations coming up again and again on each list. The only surprise is when a big name is not on all the lists.

130. A sample of the wording used is: *Central Government organisations, Departments, Arms Length Bodies (ALB's) and Non-Departmental Public Bodies (NDPB's), this framework will be the mandated route for the procurement of consultancy services within scope, between £100k and £2m in value. Work below £100k and above £2m, other than by exception, will be procured via different procurement routes* (http://gps.cabinetoffice.gov.uk/contracts/rm1502).

131. Admittedly a bidder always has the right to challenge unreasonable demands by a purchaser, but it is much safer to grit teeth and comply like everyone else.

advantage, it is something that you would do well to recognise. The shift is most noticeable in the competitive dialogue process, but it can happen in the restricted procedure in the hiatus between the purchaser naming the winner and signature of the contract.

The power shift is a result of two factors: the reduction in competition as bidders are eliminated or drop out and the purchaser's deadlines which astute bidders can use for leverage. At worst a potential contractor can hint at withdrawal if concessions are not made and the purchaser is faced with the horrifying prospect of not only losing its carefully chosen winning bidder but also the whole procurement project on which so much time and effort has been expended[132].

A purchaser can take some of the steam out of any such demands by appointing the second-placed bidder as reserve. This is a doubtful honour and it is unlikely that any organisations boast of such 'awards' on their web sites, but it is always, albeit remotely, possible that either through accident or design[133] a winning bidder may not be able to sign the contract and the reserve is awarded the prize.

- ***Being appointed reserve bidder is an uncertain situation. If it happens to you make sure that you understand the rules, for example how long does the purchaser propose to keep you in a state of suspended animation and how will you know when that state ceases to be?***

Challenging procurements

None of this book constitutes legal advice and it is especially important to respect this caveat when reading this section. No decision to challenge a procurement decision should be taken without the advice of a lawyer who has specific knowledge of this particular area of the law and as is explained below the time available for taking that advice is very short.

The bar for success in challenging a procurement decision is set high. A feeling that you have been hard done by (and often you might have been) does not alone provide the grounds for a worthwhile challenge.

132. If not negotiation this is as close as makes no difference. It may well be forbidden by the Regulations, but the purchaser is in a very difficult position.

133. There have been cases where an organisation has submitted bids for contracts in multiple locations in national programmes and won so many that it could not manage them all.

You need evidence of malpractice and evidence that you were harmed by that malpractice. Evidence is not easy to obtain from a naturally reticent purchaser within the tight timescales allowed for initiating a challenge.

Challenging a procurement decision is a leap in the dark. It is much better to do everything you can to avoid the necessity for a challenge. It is regrettable but true that if formally challenged a public sector organisations will spend as much taxpayers' money as it takes to demonstrate its 'innocence', whereas asking *are you sure you are being completely fair here* before a decision is set in stone could well receive a sympathetic response.

- ***If you suspect errors or dirty dealings then immediately ask the purchaser to clarify its actions. You may cause the purchaser to examine its procedures and correct the flaw. If not and you challenge later at least the courts can't say that you didn't act as soon as you knew of the problem. An additional benefit is that the response of the purchaser might provide you with useful evidence for that challenge.***
- ***If something happens (whether or not it appears contrary to the Regulations) that gives an advantage to you in particular[134], think carefully. If you are awarded the contract and the award is challenged you could suffer collateral damage ranging from delay to losing the contract altogether.***

How are procurement decisions challenged?

The usual route for challenging procurement decisions is via the High Court and that is what in the main we discuss in this section.

A second route to challenging procurements is a complaint to the EU Commission under the principle expressed on the Commission's website[135]:

> *Anyone may lodge a complaint with the Commission against a Member State for any measure (law, regulation or administrative action) or practice attributable to a Member State which they consider incompatible with a provision or a principle of EU law.*

That anyone means anyone is emphasised by the further statement:

134. Or as a member of a subset of bidders.

135. http://ec.europa.eu/eu_law/your_rights/your_rights_forms_en.htm

You do not have to demonstrate a formal interest in bringing proceedings. Neither do you have to prove that you are principally and directly concerned by the infringement complained about.

All of which sounds encouraging, except that if you are actually seeking redress then the Commission goes on to advise you to use your national courts.

Specifically for the NHS there is a third route for challenge by making a complaint via the Co-operation and Competition Panel[136] (CCP) route. The CCP procedure is typical of complaints procedures for most public sector organisations. It begins with an attempt at 'local resolution' followed by an appeal, then a further appeal to the CCP itself. The process is held to be less formal than legal proceedings[137], but nevertheless commissioning bodies involve their legal advisors in the hearings[138] and use their advice to counter the complainant's case.

The CCP does not have the powers of the courts, particularly with regard to contracts. It makes well-meaning pleas for the signing process to be suspended while a complaint is considered, but there is little evidence (admittedly on the basis of a small number of decided complaints) that purchasers comply. In fact it is in the purchaser's interests to push on. Presenting prospective challengers with a fait accompli effectively raises the stakes because, whatever else it might do, the CCP is unable to overturn a contract once awarded.

Figures for the success of local level resolution and first-level appeals are not readily available[139], but the CCP records show that it has never yet

136. The CCP was established in 2009 with a broad remit to rule on possible breaches of the NHS's Principles and rules of co-operation and competition. Procurement disputes are generally considered under principles 1 and 2 (Principle 1: commissioners must commission services from the providers who are best placed to deliver the needs of their patients and populations. Principle 2: commissioning and procurement must be transparent and non-discriminatory and follow the Procurement guide for commissioners of NHS-funded services issued in July 2010). Following the reorganisation decreed by the NHS and Social Care Act 2012 the CCP, although still called a panel, on 1 April 2013 became Monitor's Co-operation and Competition Directorate.

137. Note that the CCP will not accept complaints that are already the subject of legal action.

138. Not that there is a hearing in the usual sense of the word, i.e. where the complainant can appear and put its case, until and unless the challenge reaches the CCP. Until this point the hearings are closed sessions of the complained-about organisation which consider written submissions from the complainant.

139. The purchaser or its superior body is judge and jury in its own case until the appeal reaches the

found for an appellant (bidder)[140]. If a bidder has suffered financial loss or disadvantage because of an unfair NHS procurement then it is doubtful that the CCP route is a sensible way to obtain compensation[141]. Worse still, by going down that route initially, the bidder risks timing itself out for a legal challenge.

The effect of Monitor's absorption of the CCP is not yet clear, but it is unlikely to prove any more of a check on poor procurement practice or to be of more commercial use to bidders than it has been in the past.

Who can challenge a procurement?

With the exception of the European Commission route, prospective challengers must have an interest in the procurement (and the resources to mount a challenge). Essentially, this means that challenges are likely to come from either bidders who took part in some or all of the process and have been unsuccessful or prospective bidders who would have taken part if they had not been barred or misled.

Typical grounds for complaints from those who have been prevented from bidding might include: unreasonable restrictions on the class of persons allowed to bid; misrepresentation of the requirement (either initially or by changing it during the course of the procurement process); failure to advertise the opportunity openly; or failure to open the opportunity to competition at all.

What is an Alcatel period?

The Alcatel[142] period is the 'standstill' period of ten (or fifteen) days[143]

CCP. No purchaser wishes to admit error and no superior body wishes to admit that its supervision was wanting.

140. However at the time of writing the CCP has only ruled on five procurement disputes.

141. CCP rules say that if the Panel finds for the appellant (bidder) it can recommend 'such remedies as it sees fit'. There is however, no indication that the remedy will be in the form of damages. Furthermore the CCP appears to be unable to prevent the signing of contracts while a procurement is in dispute. The worst possible result is success at an intermediate stage on the route. Being told that you were wronged, but there is nothing to be done because the contract has already been signed is no help to anyone, even if the finding is accompanied by the hoary old formula *lessons will be learned.*

142. The requirement for an Alcatel period does not apply to Part B services; however most purchasers of health services will observe an Alcatel period as best practice.

143. Ten days if the information was sent electronically and fifteen if it was sent by post. This is Euro-time so things like working and non-working days and day of despatch as opposed to day of receipt add further complications to time calculations during the Alcatel period.

between the purchaser naming the successful bidder and the contract being signed. The name arises from decisions in a case in the European Court involving the Alcatel telecommunications company.

The Alcatel period is initiated by the purchaser sending a letter (the Alcatel letter) informing bidders of the award decision. It tells bidders their score, the winning bidder's score, the *characteristics and relative advantages of the successful tender*[144] and the date on which the Alcatel period ends. The intention is that this information should be sufficient for each unsuccessful bidder to understand why it was not awarded the contract (and by implication understand whether it was dealt with fairly).

Whether this is the effect or not[145] does, of course, depend on the frankness of the purchaser and the degree of detail provided. In the absence of any evidence of glaring errors in arithmetic the chance of an Alcatel letter alone providing the basis for a challenge is slim.

Setting aside totally irrational behaviour on the part of the purchaser, an argument with the scores themselves (i.e. the judgement of the evaluators) is unlikely to provide grounds for challenge. There remains the remote possibility, however, that the contents of the Alcatel letter will contradict either the bidder's experience of the process or the purchaser's stated intentions at the beginning of the process, so providing a pointer to matters worthy of investigation.

If an unsuccessful bidder does go to court before the end of the Alcatel period, the purchaser is automatically stayed from entering into the contract and the bidder can apply for some or all of various remedies including: rectification of a flawed process; the excluded bidder to be included in or restored to the process; the contract to be properly awarded; or damages.

Given the challenge of assembling the necessary evidence the Alcatel period is a short time for a losing bidder, but it isn't the absolute time limit and legal action can be initiated after the end of the period. Once the contract

144. These are the main points. Consult the Public Contracts (Amendment) Regulations 2009 (http://www.legislation.gov.uk/uksi/2009/2992/contents/made) themselves or a lawyer for the full requirement. How much detail must be provided on how the score was arrived at is debatable (i.e. must the score for each question be provided) and, for the usual reason of 'commercial confidence', it is unlikely that a purchaser will feel obliged to say much about the score awarded for the bid price.
145. Still less of any comfort!

has been signed the remedies available are either damages or having the contract declared *ineffective*, which means that the courts can set aside a contract that has already been entered into[146].

The time limits for action are not generous: 30 days from the unsuccessful bidder learning of the grounds for action for damages (extendable in exceptional circumstances to three months) and six months for ineffectiveness, but if an Alcatel letter of the proper format has been sent or a contract award notice published in the OJEU then this limit is reduced to 30 days[147].

The idea behind the Alcatel period is well meaning, but it introduced further legal technicalities into what was already a complex situation. The best advice that can be given here about the use of the Alcatel period is:

- ***If the Alcatel letter raises any suspicions of wrongdoing, and if you can afford it, consult a lawyer as soon as possible.***
- ***If you are reluctant to engage a lawyer then you must act quickly. Study the Alcatel letter carefully and look for hints of inequity, errors in the process or evidence contradicting your experience of the process.***
- ***Because the Alcatel letter, in theory, provides all the information that used to be provided in what was known as an 'accelerated debriefing' these (usually) face-to-face debriefings are no longer required by the Regulations, but if the Alcatel letter does raise questions then ask for further information either in the form of a face-to-face debriefing or in writing (but be wary of being drawn into the FOIA process – the purchaser could string this out well beyond the time limits).***
- ***If you find evidence or have strong suspicions, then think carefully about how much further you can take matters without legal assistance.***

I was excluded at the PQQ stage – have I the right to know why?

Yes. The right of bidders eliminated at the PQQ stage to be informed were

146. Ineffectiveness is a new concept in English law and its full significance has yet to be fully tested. It already seems clear, however, that it is a remedy that the courts will grant in only the most exceptional circumstances.

147. This is a brief and high level summary of the time limits and should not be considered as a comprehensive guide to the law.

retro-fitted as Regulation 29A[148] by The Public Contracts (Amendment) Regulations 2009.

Essentially the same information must be provided as for unsuccessful bidders at the tender stage, but at the PQQ stage there is no time limit for sending out the notification. Nevertheless it would be a nonsense for purchasers to delay notification because any potential challenges need to be known about before the ITT is issued. If a bidder were to respond to a notice of exclusion with what was clearly a valid objection, and the ITT had already been issued, it would throw the process into disarray.

- ***If you are eliminated at the PQQ stage ask for the information to which you are entitled and check it in the same way as you would an Alcatel letter.***

What are the grounds for challenge?

Broadly put an unsuccessful bidder has grounds for challenging the award of a contract if the overarching principles of equitable treatment, transparency or non-discrimination have been breached or procedural requirements of the Regulations have not been followed and the bidder has been disadvantaged as a result. For example (and this is by no means a comprehensive list) where the purchaser:

- places unreasonable restrictions on who may take part in the procurement process;
- issues a contract notice that is at odds with the actual requirement;
- confuses the selection process (PQQ/short-listing stage) with the award process (ITT stage) by further evaluation of the bidder (rather than the bid) at the ITT stage;
- has not operated the evaluation methodology in the way defined, for example it has fiddled the numbers or just got the sums wrong;
- uses evaluation criteria that have not been revealed in the documents;
- uses perverse evaluation criteria;
- shortens the timetable part-way through the process;
- attempts to negotiate with bidders; or

148. 29A.—(1) *Where a contracting authority decides, prior to the stage at which it makes a decision to which regulation 32(1) (award decision) applies, to exclude an applicant, the contracting authority shall notify the applicant of that exclusion.*

- is partial in the provision of information, i.e. one or more bidders is put on the inside track.

Matters to consider before challenging a procurement decision

If it is your aim to improve your commercial position, then the courts are the only effective recourse. It hardly needs saying that action in the High Court does not come cheap and anyone contemplating it has to put up a considerable sum initially and face the risk of losing a lot more. Some of the factors that you need to consider are listed below.

- Can you show that you have been disadvantaged[149]? If not you are most unlikely to gain anything worthwhile whether or not there have been heinous transgressions by the purchaser[150].
- Is there a reasonable chance that you can achieve a result of commercial value to you? If not, why bother?
- Are you in a position to benefit? You might be if you had come second and the purchaser's transgression had benefitted only the winner or if you alone had been harmed, but what if the transgression harmed other bidders? Might one of them benefit more than you would from your challenge?
- Will it harm you in future procurements if you are seen as difficult? Of course it will not, except that here we are talking of the real world. On the one hand you could benefit from demonstrating that you are not to be messed about; on the other it cannot be denied that there is a degree of subjectivity an evaluation process.
- What if the purchaser invokes the nuclear option, i.e. cancels the procurement altogether or restarts it in a different guise? Your fox is shot and in reality there is not a lot you can do about it except seek compensation for your wasted time.
- Can you get the information you need in time? Some information will come from your experience of the process and the Alcatel letter, but will it be enough? If you try to ask follow up questions[151] the purchaser might invoke the FOIA.

149. i.e. if what you allege went wrong prevented you from winning, or was at least a significant hindrance?

150. You might, however, consider reporting the matter to the EU commission *pour encourager les autres*.

151. By the time the award is announced the purchaser will probably have closed the clarification process.

- Are you in time? Time is definitely of the essence in arriving at any decision and before committing yourself to any course of action you should take legal advice on this point.
- Is it worth the risk, money and effort or would you do better to learn lessons and apply them to another procurement elsewhere?

<u>What to look for</u>

None of the factors below (which should not be considered a complete or exclusive list) necessarily constitute grounds for challenge in themselves, but they do suggest that further investigation of the process might be appropriate (whether or not useful evidence would be revealed by the purchaser is another matter).

- Was any bidder allowed to make a late submission?
- Was any bidder allowed to resubmit a question?
- Did everyone receive the same information at the same time?
- Were there any unpublished evaluation guidelines?
- Was a coherent and robust evaluation methodology described in advance of or with the PQQ/ITT?
- Was the process, especially the evaluation, conducted in the way that the bidder said it would be[152]?
- How were the results of the presentations actually incorporated into the final score?
- Was there a pre-set protocol for presentations? Were you told about it and was it followed in all cases?
- Was the matching of answers to evaluators consistent? (e.g. were questions 1 – 6 in all submissions marked by Smith or did Jones help out with some submissions?)
- Were evaluators required to record reasons for their scores?
- If not why not?
- If they were then are the records available?
- Do their reasons make sense?
- Do the reasons given comply with the evaluation guidelines?
- Did the contract let at the end of the process reflect the requirements set out at the beginning, including the description of the requirement in the contract notice?

152. If there were some changes to the process along the way, but all bidders were told and no one objected at the time then there is probably no case to answer.

Why do purchasers fear a challenge?

Only a brave and well-resourced bidder standing on solid legal ground is likely to go to the High Court to challenge an award, so it seems strange that the fear of challenge looms over a purchaser's every decision. However if purchasers were to articulate their fears they would probably acknowledge[153] that what really scares them is that unlikely as a challenge might be its consequences are profound.

Whether successful or not, a challenge brings bad publicity, expense, the discomfort of being involved in legal proceedings and, depending on circumstances, delays in signing the contract. A successful challenge could add to these (any or all of) re-running all or part of the procurement process, having the contract declared ineffective and a fine.

None of these consequences are comfortable and some could be, in the unfortunate modern jargon, career limiting for those held to be responsible.

It is impossible to know within the NHS context whether challenge through the CCP route is seen by purchasers as a distinct additional threat, or even whether it figures at all. Given that the threshold to taking action is lower, i.e. the bidder can pursue the challenge without a lawyer and without the risk of legal costs, a complaint via the CCP route would seem to be an additional deterrent against bad procurement practice, but to date there is little or no evidence that it has this effect.

How can the risk of challenge be reduced?

When in doubt the wise purchaser seeks to do what is equitable, non-discriminatory and transparent.

It takes care to follow the rules, document all actions, record reasons for all decision (including evaluation scores) and when problems arise deals with them sympathetically and quickly. It is better to admit to a mistake and re-run a step of the procurement than face a challenge at the end, although that is not the way that all purchasers see it.

- ***If you find yourself being brought back into a procurement because a purchaser has discovered (or you have demonstrated) that you were unreasonably excluded you are entitled to continued***

153. Of course there are purchasers who overestimate the probability of a challenge, perhaps because of unfamiliarity with the procurement process.

equitable treatment, which might mean, for example, that the purchaser must extend the timetable for you whilst sticking to the original timetable for other bidders*[154]*.

- ***If you are contesting exclusion, remember that one of the most powerful factors working against you will be the purchaser's reluctance to hold up its timetable and miss a vital deadline.***

If you find yourself in the happy situation of being selected as the successful bidder you have as much, if not more, reason to avoid or head off a challenge as does the purchaser. Circumstances do not always allow, but wherever possible you should consider the following.

- ***Ensure that the content and method of service of the Alcatel notice is compliant with the Regulations, because errors here are grounds for challenge in themselves.***
- ***Insist on signing the contract as soon as possible after the end of the Alcatel period because signature starts the clock ticking for time limitation of challenges.***
- ***Insist that the purchaser publishes the contract award notice in the OJEU as soon as possible. Although it has always been a requirement of the Regulations, at one time many purchasers didn't bother to publish the notice and there were no consequences. With the amendments of 2009*[155] *the notice now also starts the clock ticking for time limitation of challenges.***
- ***Draw up an agreement with the purchaser (becoming known as a 'pre-nuptial agreement') setting out procedures for unwinding the contract should it be rendered ineffective through no fault of your own.***

You could find yourself the innocent victim of a challenge even when there was no procurement process, because there are circumstances where a rival supplier could challenge for that very reason.

- ***If you are operating under a contract to provide public services and changes are proposed you need to consider whether these changes are substantial, in which case the courts might hold that provision must be opened up to competition.***

---

154. By, for example, accepting everyone else's submissions and putting them into cold storage until yours arrives.

155. The Public Contracts (Amendment) Regulations 2009

- ***Similarly if there are proposals to extend or renew your existing contract for the provision of public services then you need to confirm that the extension or renewal complies with the Regulations and was provided for in the initial procurement process.***

Some technicalities concerning contracts

This section is far from being a treatise on the law of contract, but it might be helpful to explain a few points that have been known to confuse both purchasers and bidders.

Structure

A contract[156] comes in two parts – the body and the schedules. Confusingly, some people refer to the body as the contract and the schedules as the schedules as if they were somehow of less significance, but this can't be helped.

Despite the enthusiasm of lawyers for producing new contracts for every occasion most service contracts have similar underlying structures and their bodies tend to cover broadly the same grounds using broadly the same words and phrases. In general, the main difference between service contracts lies in the contents (but not necessarily titles) of their schedules. It is in the schedules where (generally) matters specific to the particular service are addressed and where, for example, the service definition and the performance regime are likely to be defined[157].

Draft contract

Purchasers tend to issue a draft contract early in the procurement process. The purpose of doing so is to allow the bidders to understand the main obligations they would be taking on and the main terms and conditions that would apply.

The specifics, such as names, dates, location of premises, prices, are left blank but it would be reasonable to expect matters such as contract duration and (possibly) extension period; pricing elements, performance regime; and

156. By which is meant the document that sets out the agreement. Contract can also mean an agreement made between two or more parties with the intention of it being legally enforceable and involving the exchange of consideration, etc (i.e. the legal concept of a contract as opposed to a physical document). It is to be hoped that the context makes clear which meaning is intended where.
157. But there is no particular reason why these specifics should not appear in the body of the contract and some of them sometimes do.

the major characteristics of the service to be defined (more or less) in full.

The content of the draft contract forms some or all of the specification of the purchaser's requirement so any substantive[158] change between draft and final contract would be contrary to the Regulations and would open the procurement to challenge.

Contract period

With certain exceptions such as NHS dental contracts, service contracts will have a limited period of validity. The general view is that for any service that requires the contractor to expend significant time, effort and expense in setting it up the minimum reasonable period is five years. A shorter period would mean that the annual cost would be overly boosted by the recovery of the setting-up costs; not only that, the contractor would have only a short time to settle in before it was time for the purchaser to begin the procurement process again.

The cost of frequent re-procurement should not be ignored. The successful bidder will look to recover its bidding costs[159] from the contract price and the procurement process itself is a cost to the purchaser, so it is in the interests of neither to repeat the procurement too frequently.

The maximum length for a service contract is held to be around seven years[160]. A longer period could be criticised or even subjected to legal challenge on the grounds that it stifles competition. From the point of view of the purchaser too long a contract period risks the suitability and commercial viability of the service as defined being eroded by a changing environment.

Optional extensions

Purchasers often write an optional extension period into a service contract, but are not always entirely sure what it means or indeed what it is for[161].

158. 'Substantive' is the author's coinage, not a legal usage specific to these circumstances. What is substantive? Its all a matter of opinion, but if, say, the required location for the delivery of services was changed from one end of a short street to the other this might not be substantive, but if the location was changed from one town to another it possibly would be.

159. And commercial reality dictates the bidder must also recover the costs of all those other bids in which it was unsuccessful.

160. Although some service contracts such as rail franchises have even longer periods to allow recovery of the very large capital investments involved.

161. At the time of writing it into the contract they are unsure, but when it comes to renewal views harden. In the author's experience extension clauses are invoked (and gratefully accepted by the

Intriguing discussions can take place along the lines of: *can't we have a seven-year contract with an option for us to cancel after five?*

To which the purchaser's advisor replies: *then what you are asking for is a five year contract with an optional two-year extension. Any bidder in its right mind would price for a five year contract and treat an extra two years as a bonus*. The purchaser's response to this advice usually starts: *yes, but...*

A provision for extending a contract can sensibly only be based on mutual agreement, i.e. at the end of the initial contractual period either side can pull out without penalty or criticism if they wish to.

It has to be recognised that a contract extension is potentially a way of re-procuring a service without going through a competitive process. For this reason it is generally accepted that the extension period should be less than half of the initial contract period (five years with a two year extension – *5 plus 2* in the jargon – is common).

Any substantive change in the terms of the contract when extended, such as the scope of services or the rates of payment[162], would also fall foul of the Regulations on the grounds that it was effectively a new service[163].

- ***If you are preparing to sign a contract with an extension clause, ensure that: a) the clause complies with the Regulations; b) you understand your rights and obligations under the clause; and c) the purchaser doesn't have unreasonable expectations of what the clause means.***

Contracts can't override law

It is a well established legal principle that the law of the land takes precedence over anything said in a contract. This was demonstrated by the case of Dr Eddie Crouch[164], an orthodontist who in 2008 successfully established in court that his contract could not be unilaterally terminated by South Birmingham Primary Care Trust because the secondary legislation governing the contract said otherwise.

---

contractor) more often than not because purchasers are usually slow off the mark in starting re-procurement.

162. Unless already provided for in the contract by, for example, price indexation.

163. Nevertheless, provisions for contract extension are pushed to the limit, and sometimes beyond, by purchasers who put off the re-procurement exercise until it is too late.

164. Crouch v South Birmingham PCT

Commencement of contract/service

There are two terms that appear in a service contract (and perhaps the ITT or other procurement documents) that must be used with care because they can lead to confusion: *contract commencement date* and *service commencement date*[165].

Contract commencement date is the date on which the contract is signed by the parties, i.e. the date when purchaser and successful bidder (who by signing becomes the contractor) commit themselves in law to deliver their respective responsibilities as defined in the contract. The principal commitment on the part of the contractor will be to provide the service to the required standard and on the part of the purchaser it will be to pay the contractor for doing so.

Frequently, a contract is signed, i.e. commences, some time before delivery is required to commence because the contractor, particularly if it is a new contractor or a new service, has to make various preparations and requires the protection of a contract before committing to the expense thereof[166].

Purchasers talk of a *five-year contract* and generally mean that they wish the services to be delivered for a period of five years, not say, six months of mobilisation followed by four-and-a-half years of service delivery. It is important, therefore to distinguish between the *contract commencement date* and the *service commencement date* which marks the beginning of service delivery, its measurement and payment.

- ***Ensure sure that you, and the purchaser, understand the difference between contract commencement date and service commencement date as early as possible in the procurement, otherwise you may be pricing for a five year contract but will only receive four-and-a-half years of revenue.***

Do statements made in a response to an ITT become part of the contract?

Although some purchasers believe that they do, as a general rule anything said in a response to a PQQ or ITT is without contractual significance unless it is specifically written into the agreement itself[167].

165. Or variations such as *date of commencement* and *commencement of service date*.
166. Often called mobilisation and includes such activities as finding and setting up premises, establishing processes, recruiting staff, dealing with TUPE matters. Even if an incumbent wins a re-procurement it will usually have some preparation works to do.
167. This is usually be done by adding parts of the bidder's response as a schedule to the contract. A

Contracts usually contain an *entire agreement* clause stating that the agreement between the parties consists solely of what is says in the contract and that anything else that might have been said or written during the process leading up to signing the contract, or at any other time for that matter, is irrelevant unless it is written into that contract.

- ***An ITT asks you to describe innovative ways of delivering services. You put forward a brilliant, but (as it later becomes clear) expensive set of proposals for innovations and you win the bid. Don't panic, there is no obligation on you to deliver the proposed innovations unless they are specifically written in the contract.***
- ***Nevertheless, if you have any doubts about what the contract commits you to then take legal advice.***

Exit plan

Most service contracts contain a section, usually a schedule, called an exit plan. This sets out the obligations on both sides in the period leading up to, during, and for a period after the termination[168] of the contract, including, but not necessarily limited to:

- managing handover to a successor contractor in an efficient manner avoiding unnecessary cost;
- providing information to competitors and/or the purchaser such as employment records of staff, manuals and procedures, information required for TUPE purposes;
- making staff available for interview by competitors;
- allowing access to premises;
- handing over premises in good condition;
- ensuring relevant sub-contracts entered into by the contractor are transferrable (can be novated to use the jargon) to a successor contractor;
- maintaining the services at the required standard up to (and perhaps in the case of delays to the procurement beyond) the termination date;
- returning relevant assets to the purchaser;

typical such addition would be a mobilisation plan or delivery schedule that the bidder has supplied with the tender.

168. The exit plan will (must!) cover both *termination by the effluxion of time* – the delightful legal phrase that means the contract has run its (five-year or whatever) course – and prior termination for reasons such as breach by one side or the other.

- returning confidential information and properly disposing of any copies thereof; and
- transferring licences, special equipment, etc to a successor contractor.

Usually the purchaser requires obligations under an exit plan to be fulfilled at no additional cost, although depending on the contractor's own financial arrangements charges might apply to the transfer of licences, special equipment, etc.

- ***If you are bidding in the re-procurement of a service contract ask to see the existing exit plan and use it to assess your risks at handover and set-up.***
- ***If there is no exit plan defined ask the purchaser for a policy statement covering the topics usually contained in an exit plan.***
- ***Consider asking the purchaser for an indemnity against either purchaser or incumbent falling down on their responsibilities under the exit plan.***
- ***If you win the contract don't forget that you may have to execute your own exit plan at the end of the contract period, so keep it under constant review.***

Responding to PQQs and ITTs

Some at least of what follows can be characterised as blindingly obvious. Nevertheless, anyone who has ever run a procurement will tell you that it is not so to every bidder.

- ***Evaluators generally carry out their duties alongside their day job or even when they get home in the evening. Take it from someone who had done his share of evaluation – it is grindingly boring and far from enjoyable, so don't make things even worse for evaluators by ignoring the purchaser's rules for submission.***
- ***Although most evaluators will strive to be fair to all bidders, they are only human. If you try their patience you may erode their sense of fairness, at least as far as your bid is concerned.***
- ***Read the instructions about how to make your submission, then read them again, then OBEY THEM. When you have prepared your submission check it again specifically to make sure that you have obeyed the instructions.***

- ***Some submissions look as if they were written by several different people, each of whom expected someone else to take overall responsibility. If more than one person is involved then appoint an editor and give him or her the time, resources and authority to do the job properly.***
- ***Study the purchaser's rules carefully along with any evaluation criteria, scoring guidance, evaluation methodology, etc. Look for easy ways to score points and obvious ways to avoid losing them.***
- ***If there are words limits then OBEY THEM. They are not imposed for fun and anything beyond the word limit will be ignored. Use the word count facility in your word processor – it's not difficult, but it's surprising how few bidders can make it work.***
- ***On the other hand don't treat the word limit as a target; it is usually no more than the purchaser's best guess of how many words you will need. Use enough words to say what you have to say and don't pad out your answer with waffle.***
- ***If an answer goes over the word limit see how many words you can get rid of without losing sense and content demanded by the question. If you still can't squeeze in under the limit, ask the purchaser whether it can raise the limit. If the purchaser agrees the concession will apply to every bidder.***
- ***Even if your answers don't exceed the word limit eliminate waffle by following the advice in the first sentence of the point above.***
- ***If you are answering a multi-part question make sure that you specifically address each part.***
- ***Similarly, if evaluation guidance has been published, make sure that your answer addresses and satisfies every point identified in the guidance.***
- ***Use jargon and abbreviations with care – the evaluator may not know them or their meaning may be ambiguous.***
- ***If there are specific requirements to be satisfied in your answers then make sure that you meet them. Hoping that something will do is not enough***[169]***.***

169. The location of premises in a designated geographical area is an example of a specific requirement. Your chosen location is either in the designated area or outside it. Outside, but quite near will not wash. These things are not difficult to check!

- ***Points are only awarded for what you write down, so don't skimp on an answer on the grounds that everyone knows this so I don't need to explain.***
- ***With a little care and thought you should be able to guarantee full marks on some questions. For example, if you are asked about your cardiopulmonary resuscitation procedures, provided that they are fully compliant with current best practice, only a defective description could lose marks.***
- ***If you are pushed for time concentrate first on getting the red flag questions right, then on the questions carrying the highest weightings. But remember, even one point can be a winning margin.***
- ***Just because some questions in procurements for services are similar whoever the purchaser or whatever the service don't assume that answers can be copied willy-nilly from one submission to another***[170]***. Make sure that you aim your answers at the specific purchaser.***
- ***Answer the questions that your purchaser has asked not those that you would like to answer.***
- ***If additional information or documents are requested, provide them in the format the bidder asks for, not in the format that you prefer.***
- ***Be very careful about red flag questions – you risk disqualification if you get the answer wrong or don't answer.***
- ***NEVER caveat an answer with a formula such as 'subject to further investigations on our part, we are willing to undertake to …' The only proper score for this answer is 0.***
- ***Some questions are extremely sensitive; for example, a question that often appears in either the PQQ or the ITT is 'do you accept the conditions of the draft contract***[171]*** as supplied?' There is, of***

170. The worst crime to commit when copying from another submission is failing to do a full edit of the name of the customer. It does not impress if purchaser ABC reads, for example, that the bidder has done a thorough analysis of the requirements of purchaser XYZ and proposes the following solutions which are tailored to the specific requirements of XYZ. This happens and it can be particularly embarrassing (although highly amusing from the purchaser's point of view) when the mistake is made on presentation slides.

171. Assuming of course that the purchaser has been able to supply a draft contract at the PQQ stage, but there can be other *do you accept* questions. The same advice applies to these.

course, only one answer to this question and you can't dodge it by leaving it blank or answering 'for further discussion'. Anything but 'yes' is likely to result in immediate rejection.

- ***When you think you have finished your submission check that it complies with the instructions, then check each answer carefully[172], then check them all again and if possible ask someone else to check as well. Only when you are certain that you have done your best and done it according to the purchaser's requirements should you press the (perhaps metaphorical) submit button.***
- ***Finally, and this applies throughout the procurement process, not just to making your responses, don't automatically assume that the purchaser knows what it is doing; it might do, but then again it might not, so never be afraid to ask for clarification.***

Can I leave my response to the last minute?

This is self-evidently a silly question, which is why it is left until the end. Nevertheless it is quite clear to anyone who has run a procurement that many bidders consider last minute submission to be an eminently sensible strategy, until they hit problems that is.

- ***Prepare your submission early, but don't submit it early – new information may become available and things may change.***
- ***On the other hand, don't submit at the last minute – that is when printers break, ink dries up, internet links fail, fuses blow, couriers lose their way, electronic procurement systems turn against you, and all sorts of other gremlins crawl out of the woodwork.***

In conclusion

This book comes with no guarantees. Following its advice will not mean that you will win the next service contract that you bid for, but it will undoubtedly improve your chances and the biggest gains will be made by following the most basic advice. Never forget what you were told at school

172. For example, an unfinished sentence neither impresses nor scores points, and if the part that is missing is an explanation of your financial standing, it matters not how big your organisation is. You are judged on your answer, not on your reputation and you will be rejected (this has happened!)

before an exam: *write neatly and read the instructions at the top of the paper before you start.*

Bibliography

<u>**CCP**</u>
Publisher: Monitor
Date of page: No date
Title of page: Co-operation and Competition
URL: http://www.monitor-nhsft.gov.uk/cooperationandcompetition
Date accessed: 12 July 2013

Publisher: Department of Health
Date of page: 30 July 2010
Title of page: Principles and rules for co-operation and competition
URL: https://www.gov.uk/government/uploads/system/uploads/attachment_data/file/216279/dh_118220.pdf
Date accessed: 12 July 2013

<u>**Co-operatives**</u>
Publisher: The Guardian
Date of page: 17 November 2010
Title of page: Public sector workers encouraged to form John Lewis-style co-operatives
URL: http://www.guardian.co.uk/politics/2010/nov/17/public-sector-workers-cooperatives-mutuals
Date accessed: 12 July 2013

<u>**Dental Access Programme**</u>
Publisher: Bevan Brittan
Date of page: 12 May 2010
Title of page: A little bit more on PDS Plus
URL: http://www.bevanbrittan.com/articles/Pages/AlittlebitmoreonPDSPlus.aspx
Date accessed: 12 July 2013

<u>**Equitable Access Programme**</u>
Publisher: National Archives

Date of page: 15 August 2010
Title of page: Equitable Access to Primary Medical Care services (EAPMC): procurement at PCTs
URL: http://webarchive.nationalarchives.gov.uk/+/www.dh.gov.uk/en/Aboutus/Procurementandproposals/Procurement/ProcurementatPCTs/index.htm
Date accessed: 12 July 2013

EU procurement information
Publisher: European Union
Date of page: No date
Title of page: Information about European public procurement
URL: http://simap.europa.eu/index_en.htm
Date accessed: 12 July 2013

Publisher: EU Bookshop
Date of page: 2010
Title of page: The Miniguide to Ted
URL: http://bookshop.europa.eu/is-bin/INTERSHOP.enfinity/WFS/EU-Bookshop-Site/en_GB/-/GBP/ViewPublication-Start?PublicationKey=OA3109167
Date accessed: 12 July 2013

Publisher: European Commission
Date of page: 11 June 2012
Title of page: Making a complaint
URL: http://ec.europa.eu/eu_law/your_rights/your_rights_forms_en.htm
Date accessed: 12 July 2013

Legal citations
Publisher: The Law Society Gazette
Date of page: 2010
Title of page: Public procurement rules are causing dismay among contracting authorities
URL: http://www.lawgazette.co.uk/in-practice/public-procurement-

regulations-causing-dismay-among-contracting-authorities
Date accessed: 12 July 2013

Publisher: 4-5 Gray's Inn Square
Date of page: 2008
Title of page: Case reports: R (on the application of Crouch) v South Birmingham Primary Care Trust
URL: http://www.4-5.co.uk/cases/index.cfm?id=1972
Date accessed: 12 July 2013

Publisher: Government Opportunities
Date of page: 21 June 2011
Title of page: J Varney & Sons Waste Management Ltd. V Hertfordshire County Council [2011] EWCA Civ 708
URL: http://www.govopps.co.uk/j-varney-sons-waste-management-ltd-v-hertfordshire-county-council-2011-ewca-civ-708/
Date accessed: 12 July 2013

Publisher: Practical Law Company
Date of page: 7 July 2008
Title of page: High Court finds that local authority breached procurement rules in application of award criteria
URL: http://uk.practicallaw.com/6-382-5213
Date accessed: 12 July 2013

Lottery
Publisher: Economist
Date of page: 21 December 2000
Title of page: The lottery Rolled over
URL: http://www.economist.com/node/461035
Date accessed: 12 July 2013

Procurement legislation
Publisher: The National Archives
Date of page: 2002

Title of page: The Public Contracts Regulations 2006
URL: http://www.legislation.gov.uk/uksi/2006/5/contents/made
Date accessed: 12 July 2013

Publisher: The National Archives
Date of page: 2009
Title of page: The Public Contracts (Amendment) Regulations 2009
URL: http://www.legislation.gov.uk/uksi/2009/2992/contents/made
Date accessed: 12 July 2013

TUPE
Publisher: Department for Business Innovation & Skills
Date of page: June 2009
Title of page: A guide to the 2006 TUPE Regulations for employees, employers and representatives
URL: http://www.berr.gov.uk/files/file20761.pdf
Date accessed: 12 July 2013

UK government procurement guidance
Publisher: Cabinet Office
Date of page: 2013
Title of page: Current Procurement Rules
URL: http://procurement.cabinetoffice.gov.uk/policy-capability/latest-policy-and-regulations/public-procurement-policy
Date accessed: 12 July 2013

Publisher: Cabinet Office
Date of page: 21 May 2013
Title of page: Procurement policy notes
URL: https://www.gov.uk/government/organisations/cabinet-office/series/procurement-policy-notes
Date accessed: 12 July 2013

Publisher: Government Procurement Service
Date of page: No date available

Title of page: I am a supplier
URL: http://gps.cabinetoffice.gov.uk/i-am-supplier
Date accessed: 12 July 2013

<u>**West coast main line**</u>
Publisher: HMG
Date of page: 3 October 2012
Title of page: West Coast Main Line franchise competition cancelled
URL: https://www.gov.uk/government/news/west-coast-main-line-franchise-competition-cancelled
Date accessed: 12 July 2013

Index

abandoned procurements 66–67
accounts – *see also* financial information 30, 59
adequacy 23, 40, 41, 42
Alcatel
  letter 34, 74, 75, 76
  period 73, 74, 75, 80
algorithm – *see also* Most Econonmically Advantageous Tenders 42
award 2, 6, 7, 23, 33, 43, 54, 58, 60, 63, 68, 71, 74, 75, 76, 77, 79, 80
  and Most Economically Advantageous Tender 5
  challenge an, 79, 76
  past performance 31–32

balance of power 4, 69
  shift 69
bidders 1, 3, 5, 2, 6, 7, 9, 10, 12, 16, 17, 18, 19, 20, 21, 22, 23, 24, 25, 26, 27, 28, 29, 30, 31, 32, 33, 38, 39, 40, 42, 43, 46, 53, 54, 56, 59, 61, 69, 70, 73, 74, 75, 76, 78, 79, 80, 82, 83, 84, 85, 86, 87, 88
  applying to become a bidder 9–10
  event 20, 21
  presentations 3, 53
  protocols and procedures 26
  vehicle 59, 60
bid team 64, 65
budgetary limits 24, 25
  purchaser obligation 24–26

Cabinet Office 3, 5, 15
challenging procurements 4, 70
  fears 79
  grounds for a challenge 76–77
    non-discrimination 76

how to challenge 71–72
matters to consider 77
risk reduction 79–80
the Alcatel period 73–74
what to look for 78
who can challenge? 73
clarification process 3, 20, 21, 22, 77
competitive dialogue – *see also* The Regulations 5
consortia 60
contract award notice – *see also* Award 75, 80
contract manager 52
contract notice 19, 39, 57, 76, 78
contracts
and the law 83–84
award 7, 68, 71, 74
notice 2, 75, 80
past performance 31
commencement 84
draft contracts 81–82
entire agreement 85
period 82
optional extension 82–83
service contracts 5, 15, 81, 82, 85
exit plan 85
structure 81
termination 51, 52, 85
contracts finder 9
Co-operation and Competition Panel (CCP) 72, 73, 79
customer satisfaction surveys 51

Dental Access Project 56
disaggregation 4

economic operators 38, 39
electronic procurement systems 9, 17, 19, 89
equity 3
EU Commission – *see also* challenging procurements 71
evaluation 3, 13, 14, 21, 23, 24, 25, 26, 31, 33, 34, 35, 36, 37, 38, 41, 43, 44, 45, 54, 55, 56, 57, 58, 64, 76, 77, 78, 79, 86, 87
 criteria 3, 26, 34, 35, 36, 37, 38, 56, 76
 methodology 36, 43, 76, 78, 87
 sub-criteria 35, 36
evaluators – *see also* evaluation criteria 3, 13, 14, 26, 30, 31, 34, 35, 36, 37, 38, 40, 53, 54, 63, 65, 74, 78, 86
 and project managers 34
expression of interest – *see also* Contract Notice 9

financial and economic standing 17, 39, 40, 41, 57, 59, 60, 89
financial information 30, 39
financial schedules 46
framework agreement 4, 67, 68
Freedom of Information Act (FOIA) 25, 26, 27, 75, 77

Government Procurement Service 67

High Court 71, 77, 79

incumbent supplier – *see also* TUPE 61, 62, 63, 66
indemnity 86
Information Commissioner 26, 27
innovation 56
Invitation to Tender (ITT) 3, 2, 6, 14, 16, 17, 20, 23, 24, 25, 29, 30, 31, 33, 34, 35, 36, 39, 42, 43, 44, 45, 51, 53, 54, 56, 58, 65, 66, 68, 76, 78, 84, 85, 88
 award 23
 award stage 54, 56, 58, 60, 88

elephant traps 30
evaluating complex costs
Variable annual price 44–45
Volume-related pricing 43–44
response
missing information 27
short-listing 3, 5, 23, 38, 39, 40, 76
law of unintended consequences 41
statements in response 84–85
contractual significance 84

legal personality – *see also* bidders 59
loopholes 45

Maude, Francis 15
mini-competition – *see also* Framework Agreement 68
Most Economically Advantageous Tender (MEAT) 5, 6

National Lottery 62
negotiated procedure – *see also* The Regulations 5, 28
negotiation 5, 28, 29, 30, 55, 70
NHS Principles of Co-operation and Competition 72

Official Journal of the European Union (OJEU) 2, 4, 5, 8, 9, 12, 14, 67, 68, 75, 80
Open procedure – *see also* The Regulations 5
output-based approach 56

past performance 3, 31
performance indicators 3, 48
performance regime 48, 81
Pre-qualification Questionnaire (PQQ) 3, 2, 6, 16, 17, 20, 23, 24, 25, 30, 33, 34, 35, 36, 40, 41, 42, 43, 53, 54, 56, 58, 59, 60, 65, 68, 75, 76,

78, 84, 88
award 23
selection 23
price ceiling 3, 24, 25, 31, 42, 45, 46
price score 31, 43
pricing
Variable annual price 44
Volume-related pricing 43–44
principles of public procurement 3
Private Finance Initiative (PFI) 47
procurement
context 11
failure of common sense 15
ignorance of The Regulations 15
organisational process 14
paralysis by (legal) analysis 13
scope of the Regulations 12
shortage of experience 12
shortage of resource 13
skills gap 12
the tyranny of deadlines 13
uncertainty about numbers 13
procurement hub 10
procurement process
negotiation 5–6, 28–29, 29–30, 30–31, 55–56, 70–71
project manager 34, 52, 53, 65
protocols and procedures 26
Public Contracts (Amendment) Regulations 2009 74, 76, 80
Public Contracts Regulations (2006) 17
punitive charges 51

qualifying thresholds – *see also* The Regulations 4
quality 7, 13, 14, 23, 24, 31, 35, 40, 41, 42, 43, 53, 54

score 7, 31, 42, 43, 54
questions
characteristics of the bidder or service 53
problem with, 52
red flag 34

remedies 73, 74
re-procurement 66, 82, 83, 84, 86
cost of, 82
reserve bidder 70
restricted procedure – *see also* Regulations 5, 6, 68
risk sharing 3, 47

selection 23, 33, 38, 39, 43, 52, 54, 58, 59, 60, 69, 76
service level 46
services
Part A 7, 8
Part B 3, 7, 8, 9, 73
set-up costs 44, 62, 64
short-listing
and financial capability 39
and first stage exclusion 39
and technical ability 39
short-listing – *see also* Invitation to Tender (ITT) 3, 5, 23, 38, 39, 40, 76
Small and Medium Enterprises (SMEs) 57
Supply2health 9

Tenders Electronic Daily (TED) 8
The Regulations 1, 2, 3, 4, 7, 8, 9, 12, 13, 14, 15, 17, 29, 35, 38, 40, 41, 57, 58, 64, 69, 70, 71, 75, 76, 80, 81, 82, 83
award by central government departments and agencies 5
award by other public bodies 5
competitive dialogue 5

negotiated procedure 5
open procedure 5
qualifying thresholds 4
restricted procedure 5
time limits for action – *see also* Alcatel letter 75
Transfer of Undertakings (Protection of Employment) Regulations (TUPE) 2006 3, 61, 62, 64, 84, 85
Treaty of Rome 3

Variable annual price 44
Volume-related pricing 43

weightings – *see also* evaluation criteria 14, 35, 36, 88

26546218R00063

Printed in Great Britain
by Amazon